All-Time Favorite
Scrap Quilts
from That Patchwork Place®

Martingale® & COMPANY

All-Time Favorite Scrap Quilts
from That Patchwork Place®
© 2011 by Martingale & Company

 *Martingale*®
& COMPANY

That Patchwork Place® is an imprint of
Martingale & Company®.

Martingale & Company
19021 120th Ave. NE, Suite 102
Bothell, WA 98011
www.martingale-pub.com

CREDITS

President & CEO: Tom Wierzbicki

Editorial Director: Mary V. Green

Managing Editor: Tina Cook

Developmental Editor: Karen Costello Soltys

Design Director: Stan Green

Technical Editor: Nancy Mahoney

Copy Editor: Melissa Bryan

Production Manager: Regina Girard

Illustrators: Laurel Strand, Robin Strobel,
      & Adrienne Smitke

Cover & Text Designer Designer: Stan Green

Photographer: Brent Kane

Printed in China
16 15 14 13 12 11   8 7 6 5 4 3 2 1

Library of Congress Cataloging-in-Publication Data is available upon request.

ISBN: 978-1-60468-053-9

MISSION STATEMENT
Dedicated to providing quality products and
service to inspire creativity.

Contents

Introduction

Capturing every color of the rainbow, fabric scraps are like natural wonders. Quilters treasure them and measure them—and naturally wonder what to do with them. At That Patchwork Place, we have a host of scrap-quilt experts to help! Let Kim Diehl, Mimi Dietrich, Pat Speth, and other best-selling authors show you how to confidently combine scraps to bring spontaneity and excitement to your quilts. Featuring clear instructions and illustrations, these inspiring projects make it easy to create the scrap quilts you've been dreaming of.

TECHNIQUE. Turn to "Quiltmaking Basics" on page 84 for all the information you need to get started. Step by step, this section takes you through everything from rotary cutting the first piece to binding the finished quilt. Brush up on chain piecing, various appliqué techniques, cutting and applying borders, and more. As you choose from the wide variety of projects, you'll enjoy furthering your skills. For example, create "Jamie's Quilt" on page 21 and perfect the art of making half-square-triangle units. Or make "Fractured Diamonds" on page 63 and learn to sew scraps of varying widths to a fabric foundation to make a four-pointed star.

COLOR. A scrap quilt is an open invitation to play with color. Try "Lattice Make a Quilt" on page 53 and discover the different effects you can achieve with value placement. Red is a strong color that works well as the accent for this diagonal and horizontal grid pattern. "Stars over Mitford" on page 71 is another great quilt for focusing on value. You'll also find projects that illustrate what can be done with a limited color palette. Indulge in browns as delicious as cinnamon and gingerbread in "Apple Crisp" on page 59. Or gather up your greens and create "Luck of the Irish" on page 25. If you'd like a fresh approach to color that results in a charming yet modern quilt, don't miss "All in a Row" on page 11.

DESIGN. Here's your chance to impress your family and friends with striking yet doable designs. Take a look at the Depression-era "Double Windmill" on page 29 for a surprisingly easy quilt with only two pattern pieces. The delightful quilting design features swirls of "wind" to bring the windmills to life. "Good Fences Make Good Neighbors" on page 81 is a dynamic quilt that looks complex but is actually a simple block in a diagonal setting. For a lovely design that adds a touch of appliqué, treat yourself to "Vintage Memories" on page 43 or "Cherry Cobbler" on page 67.

Among these all-time favorites you'll find projects ranging from cozy lap quilts to generous bed quilts, and every design invites you to explore new combinations of color, pattern, and texture. So now, with our experts to guide you, you can stop wondering what to do with all those scraps you've been treasuring. Showcase them in a stunning quilt that makes your heart sing!

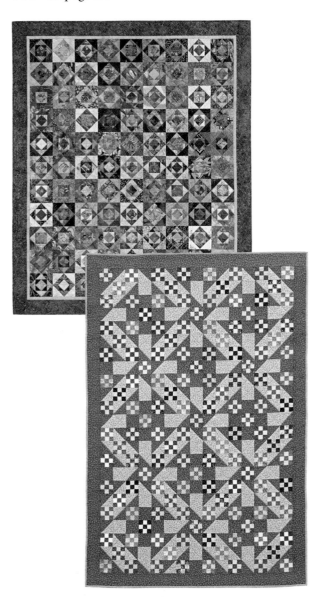

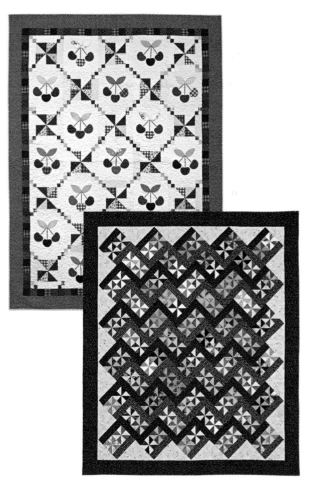

Pieced and quilted by Kim Brackett

Past and Present

The blocks in this quilt are constructed using four 6½" units. Instead of making full blocks, try experimenting with the arrangement of the smaller units to create unique settings.

Finished quilt size: 61½" x 73½"
Finished block size: 12" x 12"

Materials

Yardage is based on 42"-wide fabric.

2 yards of large-scale floral for outer border and binding

⅓ yard of blue print for inner border

40 strips (10 per color), 2½" x at least 30", of assorted dark prints in red, blue, green, and brown for blocks

40 strips, 2½" x at least 30", of assorted tan prints for blocks

4¼ yards of fabric for backing

68" x 80" piece of batting

Cutting

From *each* of the 40 assorted dark print strips and 40 assorted tan print strips, cut:

• 2 rectangles, 2½" x 6½" (a total of 80 dark and 80 tan)

• 6 squares, 2½" x 2½" (a total of 240 dark and 240 tan)

From the blue print, cut:

• 6 strips, 1½" x 42"

From the large-scale floral, cut:

• 7 strips, 6" x 42"

• 8 strips, 2½" x 42"

Making the Blocks

1. Select one 2½" x 6½" rectangle and three 2½" squares each from a single dark print and a single tan print. Layer one tan square with a dark square, right sides together and draw a diagonal line on the wrong side of the tan square. Stitch on the drawn line and trim away the excess fabric on one side, leaving a ¼" seam allowance, to make a half-square-triangle unit. Press the seam allowances toward the dark fabric.

2. Sew a tan square and a dark square to either side of the half-square-triangle unit as shown. Press the seam allowances toward the squares.

CUTTING FROM SCRAPS

To cut pieces from scraps instead of strips, use the following instructions.

From the assorted tan scraps, cut:

80 sets of:

• 1 rectangle, 2½" x 6½"

• 3 squares, 2½" x 2½"

From the assorted dark scraps, cut:

80 sets of:

• 1 rectangle, 2½" x 6½"

• 3 squares, 2½" x 2½"

See "Cutting" at left for instructions on cutting the pieces for the borders and binding.

3. Draw a diagonal line on the wrong side of a tan square. Place the marked square on one end of a dark rectangle, right sides together, as shown. Stitch on the drawn line and trim away the excess fabric, leaving a ¼" seam allowance. Press the seam allowances toward the resulting tan triangle.

4. Repeat step 3 using a dark square and a tan rectangle. Press the seam allowances toward the resulting dark triangle.

5. Join the units from steps 2, 3, and 4 to complete one-quarter of the block as shown. Press the seam allowances away from the center. Make 80 of these units.

Make 80.

6. Join one each of the red, brown, green, and blue units from step 5 to construct one block as shown. On the wrong side of the block, use a seam ripper to remove two or three stitches from the seam allowances on both sides of the center seam; then gently reposition the seam allowances to evenly distribute the fabric. Press the seam allowances in opposite directions,

opening the seam so that the center lies flat. The seam allowances should be going in a counterclockwise direction. Make 20 blocks.

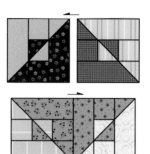 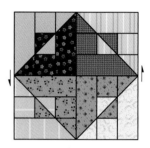

Make 20.

Assembling the Quilt Top

1. Arrange the blocks in five rows of four blocks each. Sew the blocks together in rows, pressing the seam allowances in opposite directions from row to row. Sew the rows together. Press the seam allowances in the same direction.

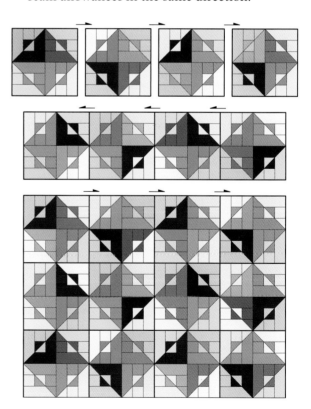

2. Sew the blue 1½"-wide strips together end to end. Referring to "Borders with Butted Corners" on page 91, measure and cut the strips, and sew them to the sides and then to the top and bottom of the quilt top for the inner border.

3. Sew the floral 6"-wide strips together end to end. Measure and cut the strips, and sew them to the quilt top for the outer border.

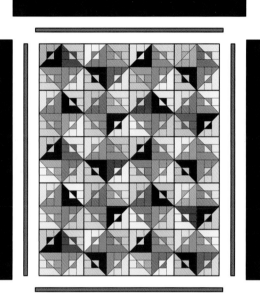

Finishing the Quilt

Refer to "Finishing" on page 93 for detailed instructions, if needed.

1. Piece the quilt backing so that it is 4" to 6" longer and wider than the quilt top.

2. Layer the quilt top with backing and batting. Baste with thread for hand quilting or with safety pins for machine quilting. If you're taking your quilt to a long-arm quilter, you do not need to layer and baste it.

3. Hand or machine quilt as desired.

4. Trim the batting and backing so that the edges are even with the quilt top. Use the floral 2½"-wide strips to bind the edges of the quilt.

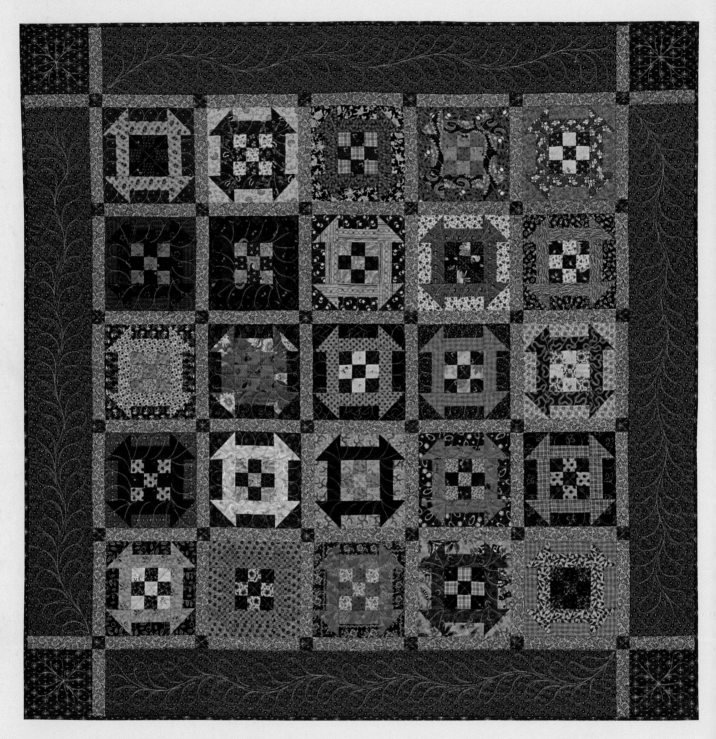

Designed by Kim Diehl; pieced by Deb Behrend; machine quilted by Celeste Freiberg

All in a Row

Combine traditional blocks with a fresh approach to color and what is the happy result? A charming yet modern quilt, revealing how old suddenly becomes new again.

Finished quilt size: 51½" x 51½"
Finished block size: 7" x 7"

Materials

Yardage is based on 42"-wide fabric.
50 "chubby sixteenths" (9" x 11") *or* 3⅝ yards *total* of assorted prints for blocks

25 squares, 6" x 6", *or* ⅞ yard *total* of assorted prints for nine-patch units

⅞ yard of dark brown print for sashing squares, border corners, and binding

¾ yard of neutral print for sashing strips

¾ yard of dark orange print for border

3¼ yards of fabric for backing

58" x 58" square of batting

Cutting

From *each* of the 25 assorted print 6" x 6" squares, cut:
- 9 squares, 1½" x 1½" (225 total)

From *each* of the 50 assorted print chubby sixteenths, cut*:
- 2 squares, 2⅞" x 2⅞" (100 total); cut each square in half diagonally to yield 2 triangles (4 total)
- 4 rectangles, 1½" x 3½" (200 total)

From the neutral print, cut:
- 14 strips, 1½" x 42"; crosscut into:
  - 60 rectangles, 1½" x 7½"
  - 8 rectangles, 1½" x 5½"

From the dark brown print, cut:
- 1 strip, 5½" x 42"; crosscut into 4 squares, 5½" x 5½"
- 6 strips, 2½" x 42"
- 2 strips, 1½" x 42"; crosscut into 36 squares, 1½" x 1½"

From the dark orange print, cut:
- 4 strips, 5½" x 39½"

For greater ease in piecing the blocks, keep the patchwork sets organized by print.

Making the Churn Dash Variation Blocks

Sew all pieces with right sides together unless otherwise noted.

1. Select four matching 1½" squares cut from one assorted print 6" square and five matching 1½" squares cut from a second assorted print 6" square. Set aside the remaining squares from each print for use when piecing the remaining nine-patch units.

2. Lay out the squares as shown to form a nine-patch unit. Join the squares in each horizontal row. Press the seam allowances of each row in alternating directions. Join the rows. Press the seam allowances in one direction.

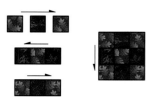

MIXING PATCHWORK PRINTS

A secret to successfully mixing many different prints is to noticeably vary the size and scale of the patterns that are placed next to each other. Whenever possible, place larger and smaller prints together, rather than positioning those of the same scale side by side. If many of your prints are of a similar size, try varying the value of the colors to achieve contrast and add further definition. When your goal is to achieve a finished quilt with a bit of the "make do" look, toss these guidelines out the window and embrace the less-than-perfect combinations that sometimes result.

3. Repeat steps 1 and 2 to make a total of 25 nine-patch units sewn from assorted pairs of prints. Each unit should measure 3½" x 3½".

4. Select a set of patchwork pieces cut from two assorted print chubby sixteenths (it isn't necessary that one set be light and one set be dark, only that the two prints are contrasting).

5. Join a 2⅞" triangle from each print along the long bias edges. Press the seam allowances to one side. Trim away the dog-ear points. Repeat to make a total of four half-square-triangle units.

Make 4 from
each pair of prints.

6. Join one 1½" x 3½" rectangle from each print as shown. Press the seam allowances to one side. Repeat to make a total of four pieced rectangle units.

Make 4 from
each pair of prints.

7. Lay out one nine-patch unit from step 3, four half-square-triangle units from step 5, and four pieced rectangles from step 6 as shown. Join the units in each horizontal row. Press the seam allowances toward the pieced rectangle units. Join the rows. Press the seam allowances toward the middle row.

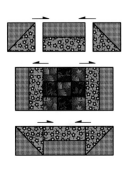 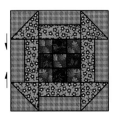

8. Repeat steps 4–7 to make a total of 25 Churn Dash Variation blocks, each measuring 7½" x 7½".

Assembling the Quilt Center

1. Lay out six dark brown 1½" squares and five neutral print 1½" x 7½" rectangles in alternating positions. Join the pieces. Press the seam allowances toward the neutral print. Repeat to make a total of six sashing rows.

Make 6.

2. Lay out six neutral print 1½" x 7½" rectangles and five Churn Dash Variation blocks in a row as shown. Join the pieces and press the seam allowances toward the neutral print. Repeat to make a total of five block rows.

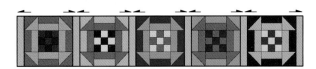

Make 5.

3. Lay out the sashing rows and block rows as shown. Join the rows. Press the seam allowances toward the sashing rows. The pieced quilt center should measure 41½" x 41½".

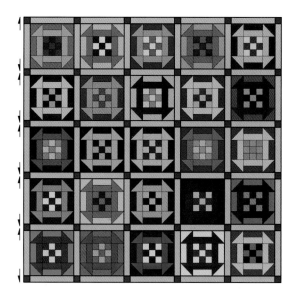

Making and Adding the Borders

1. Join a neutral print 1½" x 5½" rectangle to each end of a dark orange print 5½" x 39½" strip. Press the seam allowances toward the neutral print. Repeat to make a total of two pieced border strips. Join these strips to the right and left sides of the quilt center. Press the seam allowances toward the orange border strips.

Make 2.

2. Lay out two dark brown 5½" squares, two neutral print 1½" x 5½" rectangles, and one orange print 5½" x 39½" strip as shown. Join the pieces. Press the seam allowances toward the neutral print. Repeat to make a total of two pieced border rows. Join these rows to the remaining sides of the quilt center. Press the

seam allowances toward the orange border rows. The pieced quilt top should measure 51½" x 51½".

Make 2.

Finishing the Quilt

Refer to "Finishing" on page 93 for detailed instructions, if needed.

1. Piece the quilt backing so that it is 4" to 6" longer and wider than the quilt top.

2. Layer the quilt top with backing and batting. Baste with thread for hand quilting or with safety pins for machine quilting. If you're taking your quilt to a long-arm quilter, you do not need to layer and baste it.

3. Hand or machine quilt as desired. The blocks of the featured quilt were machine quilted with a squared feathered wreath radiating out from the seams of the center nine-patch units, and Xs were stitched onto the nine-patch centers. The sashing strips were quilted with a cable design, and the brown corner post squares were quilted with Xs. Serpentine feathered vines were quilted in the borders, and feathered Xs were quilted onto the border corner squares.

4. Trim the batting and backing so that the edges are even with the quilt top. Use the dark brown 2½"-wide strips to bind the edges of the quilt.

PORTABLE ORGANIZATION

To easily organize patchwork sets or appliqué pieces, especially for travel or classes, try layering them between paper plates. You can write special notes or instructions directly on each plate, and the plates can be stacked together to keep your work neat, compact, and easily portable.

Designed and pieced by Joanna Figueroa; quilted by Diana Johnson

My Cotswold Cottages

After Joanna spent a summer in the English district known as the Cotswolds, she wanted to capture that essence of the British countryside in a quilt. She will never forget the feeling and the scent of those cottage gardens, brimming over with nostalgic roses, delphiniums, honeysuckle, daisies, peonies, hydrangeas, foxgloves, columbine . . . and the list goes on. Here she has tried to convey with fabric what those gardens delivered to her senses.

Finished quilt size: 58" x 59"
Finished block size: 10" x 10¼"

Materials

Yardage is based on 42"-wide fabric.

⅓ yard *each* of 16 assorted medium and dark prints for houses and outer border

1⅓ yards of fabric for sashing and inner border

½ yard *each* of 3 assorted cream prints for block backgrounds and house windows

⅝ yard of fabric for binding

3⅞ yards of fabric for backing

64" x 65" piece of batting

Cutting

From *each* of the 3 cream prints, cut*:

- 2 strips, 2½" x 42"; crosscut into 24 pieces (72 total; 8 are extra), 2½" x 1¾" (A)
- 2 strips, 3½" x 42"; crosscut into 12 squares (36 total; 4 are extra), 3½" x 3½" (B)
- 2 strips, 1½" x 42"; crosscut into:
    - 6 pieces (18 total; 2 are extra), 1½" x 2½" (C)
    - 12 pieces (36 total; 4 are extra), 1½" x 3½" (D)

From *each* of the 16 medium and dark prints, cut:

- 1 strip, 2¾" x 42"; crosscut into:
    - 2 pieces (32 total), 2¾" x 4½" (E)
    - 1 piece (16 total), 2¾" x 2½" (F)
    - 2 pieces (32 total), 2¾" x 10½". Trim 1 piece to 1¾" x 10½" (G). Trim the other piece to 1¼" x 10 ½" (H).
- 1 strip, 1½" x 42"; crosscut into:
    - 2 squares (32 total), 1½" x 1½" (I)
    - 5 pieces (80 total), 1½" x 2½" (J)
- 1 strip, 3½" x 42"; crosscut into 1 piece (16 total), 3½" x 10½" (K). Set aside the remainder of this strip for the pieced outer border.

From the fabric for sashing and inner border, cut:

- 6 strips, 3½" x 42"
- 8 strips, 2½" x 42"; crosscut 4 of the strips into 12 pieces, 2½" x 10½"

From the fabric for binding, cut:

- 7 strips, 2¼" x 42"

*The amounts given are enough for 18 blocks. The excess will allow you more fabric combinations as you assemble the houses. Discard the extra pieces or set them aside for a future project.

Making the House Blocks

1. Select the pieces for one block and arrange them as shown on page 16, using pieces cut from four different fabrics to give each house its own personality. (Fold the B squares in half diagonally and place them over the ends of the K piece to mimic the finished block.) Pieces A–D should be from one fabric; pieces E, G, H, and J should be from a second fabric; pieces F and I should be

from a third fabric; and piece K should be from a fourth fabric. Repeat for each of the 16 blocks, making substitutions as necessary until you're happy with the combinations.

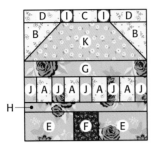

2. Separate the pieces for one block into six sections as shown.

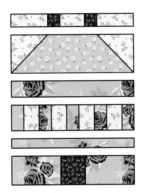

3. For the chimney section, sew the C, D, and I pieces together as shown. Press the seam allowances toward the I pieces.

4. To make the roof section, press the B squares in half diagonally, wrong sides together. With right sides together, position the squares on each end of the K piece as shown. Stitch on the pressed lines. Fold back the lower corner of each square and trim the piece(s) below them, leaving a ¼" seam allowance.

5. To make the window section, sew the A and J pieces together as shown. Press the seam allowances toward the J pieces.

6. To make the door section, sew an E piece to each side of the F piece. Press the seam allowances toward the E pieces.

7. Add the G piece to the top of the window section and the H piece to the top of the door section. Press the seam allowances toward the G and H pieces. Sew the window section to the top of the H piece. Press the seam allowances toward the H piece. Sew the roof section to the top of the G piece. Press the seam allowances toward the G piece. Join the chimney section to the top of the roof section, matching the seam intersections where the chimneys meet the roof. Press the seam allowances toward the chimney section.

Assembling the Quilt Top

1. Arrange the blocks and 2½" x 10½" sashing pieces into four vertical rows as shown. Join the blocks and sashing strips in each row. Press the seam allowances toward the sashing strips.

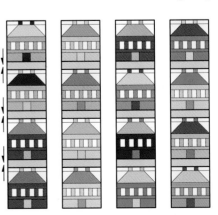

2. Measure each row through the vertical center. Each row should measure 47½", but if it doesn't, determine the average of all four rows.

3. Sew the four 2½" x 42" sashing strips together end to end to make one long strip. From the pieced strip, cut three strips to the length determined in step 2. Refer to the assembly diagram to sew these strips between the block rows. Press the seam allowances toward the sashing strips.

4. Sew the 3½"-wide inner-border strips together end to end. Referring to "Borders with Butted Corners" on page 91, measure and cut the strips, and sew them to the sides and then to the top and bottom of the quilt top.

5. To make the pieced outer border, cut the 3½"-wide medium and dark strips that you set aside previously into segments ranging from 4" to 9" long. Randomly sew the segments together, alternating medium and dark fabrics if possible, to make four outer-border strips that are at least 62" long. Press the seam allowances toward the darker of the two fabrics.

OUTER BORDER PIECING

Because this is a random border, it doesn't matter where the patches end up or what their length is.

6. Refer to "Borders with Butted Corners" to trim the strips to the length needed and sew them to the sides and then to the top and bottom of the quilt top. Press the seam allowances toward the pieced border. Once you've sewn on the border, step back and take a good look. Do you like the width of the pieced border or is it a bit too wide? Depending on your particular color combination, you might want to trim

this border to 2¾" as Joanna did. If so, use your rotary cutter and long ruler, and measure from the seam line.

Quilt assembly

Finishing the Quilt

Refer to "Finishing" on page 93 for detailed instructions, if needed.

1. Piece the quilt backing so that it is 4" to 6" longer and wider than the quilt top.

2. Layer the quilt top with backing and batting. Baste with thread for hand quilting or with safety pins for machine quilting. If you're taking your quilt to a long-arm quilter, you do not need to layer and baste it.

3. Hand or machine quilt as desired. The quilt shown has alternated stitching in the lower portion of each house, with stitching ¼" from the door, lower edges, and side edges of every other house, and an elongated X on the remaining houses. A small clamshell design was added to the roofs. The sashing and inner border features a feather design. A stipple design was used for the house backgrounds and outer border.

4. Trim the batting and backing so that the edges are even with the quilt top. Use the 2¼"-wide binding strips to bind the edges of the quilt.

Pieced by Nancy J. Martin; quilted by Fannie Mae Petersheim

Kansas Troubles

A vision in radiant reds, this quilt would be just as charming in whatever color family is calling out to be used from your stash.

Finished quilt size: 76" x 76"
Finished block size: 16" x 16"

Materials

Yardage is based on 42"-wide fabric.

2½ yards of red striped fabric for outer border

½ yard *each* of 16 assorted light prints for blocks

½ yard *each* of 16 assorted dark prints for blocks

½ yard of dark red fabric for inner border

1 yard of fabric for binding

4½ yards of fabric for backing

82" x 82" piece of batting

Cutting

From *each* of the 16 assorted light prints, cut:

- 2 squares, 5¾" x 5¾" (32 total)
- 2 squares, 8⅞" x 8⅞" (32 total); cut each square in half diagonally to yield 64 triangles
- 4 squares, 2½" x 2½" (64 total)

From *each* of the 16 assorted dark prints, cut:

- 2 squares, 5¾" x 5¾" (32 total)
- 2 squares, 4⅞" x 4⅞" (32 total); cut each square in half diagonally to yield 64 triangles
- 4 squares, 2⅞" x 2⅞" (64 total); cut each square in half diagonally to yield 128 triangles

From the dark red fabric, cut:

- 8 strips, 1½" x 42"

From the *lengthwise grain* of the red striped fabric, cut:

- 4 strips, 5¼" x 78" (Take care to cut the strips so the stripes will line up at the mitered corners.)

From the binding fabric, cut:

- 300" of 2¼"-wide bias strips

Making the Blocks

1. Use a sharp pencil and a ruler to mark two intersecting diagonal lines from corner to corner on the wrong side of each 5¾" light square. Layer the light square, right sides together, with a 5¾" dark square. Stitch ¼" from each side of both drawn diagonal lines.

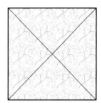

2. Cut the squares apart horizontally and vertically as shown to yield four 2⅞" squares. Then cut those squares apart on the diagonal line to yield eight half-square-triangle units. Press the seam allowances toward the dark triangle. Make a total of 256 units, 2½" x 2½".

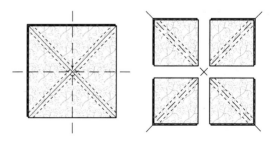

Make 8 matching units
(256 total).

3. Choosing fabrics randomly, join four half-square-triangle units, one 2½" light square, two small dark triangles, and one large dark triangle as shown.

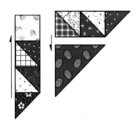 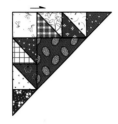

4. Join this unit to a large light triangle. Make 64 units.

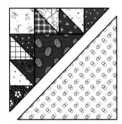 

Make 64.

5. Join four units from step 4 as shown to make a block. Make 16.

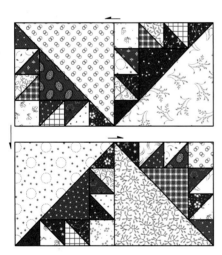

Assembling the Quilt Top

1. Arrange and sew the blocks into four rows of four blocks each. Press the seam allowances in opposite directions from row to row. Join the rows and press the seam allowances in one direction.

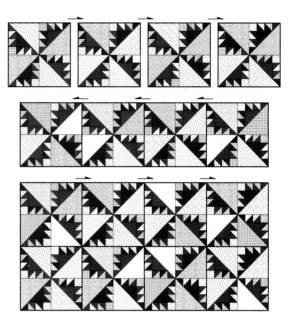

2. Sew the 1½"-wide dark red strips together end to end. Referring to "Borders with Butted Corners" on page 91, measure and cut the strips, and sew them to the sides and then to the top and bottom of the quilt top for the inner border.

3. Refer to "Borders with Mitered Corners" on page 92 to sew the 5¼"-wide strips of red striped fabric to the quilt top for the outer border.

Finishing the Quilt

Refer to "Finishing" on page 93 for detailed instructions, if needed.

1. Piece the quilt backing so that it is 4" to 6" longer and wider than the quilt top.

2. Layer the quilt top with backing and batting. Baste with thread for hand quilting or with safety pins for machine quilting. If you're taking your quilt to a long-arm quilter, you do not need to layer and baste it.

3. Hand or machine quilt as desired.

4. Trim the batting and backing so that the edges are even with the quilt top. Use the 2¼"-wide bias strips to bind the edges of the quilt.

Jamie's Quilt

This quilt features a fabulous masculine color scheme. The optical illusion adds a unique "spin" that looks difficult, but isn't. This is the perfect project for mastering your skills at making half-square-triangle units. Claudia and Le Ann named this quilt after one of the main characters in the Outlander series of books by Diana Gabaldon. Jamie was a Scottish Highlander in the eighteenth century, married to time-traveler Claire.

Finished quilt size: 68½" x 82½"
Finished block size: 12" x 12"

Materials

NICKELS
- 130 assorted cream prints for blocks (or 33 dimes)
- 65 assorted blue prints for blocks and sashing cornerstones (or 17 dimes)
- 54 assorted brown prints for blocks (or 14 dimes)

FAT QUARTERS
- 6 assorted blue prints for blocks and outer border
- 4 assorted brown prints for blocks and sashing

ADDITIONAL FABRIC AND SUPPLIES
- 1⅓ yards of brown print for inner border, corner squares, and binding
- 5 yards of fabric for backing
- 75" x 89" piece of batting

Cutting

From the 4 assorted brown print fat quarters, cut a total of*:
- 31 rectangles, 2½" x 12½"
- 16 nickel squares, 5" x 5" (add to the 54 brown nickels for blocks)

From the 6 assorted blue print fat quarters, cut a total of*:
- 18 rectangles, 5½" x 15½"
- 18 nickel squares, 5" x 5" (add to the 65 blue nickels for blocks)

From each of 50 assorted cream print nickels, cut:
- 4 squares, 2½" x 2½" (200 total)

From each of 40 assorted cream print nickels, cut:
- 2 rectangles, 2" x 3½" (80 total)

From each of 40 assorted cream print nickels, cut:
- 2 rectangles, 2" x 5" (80 total)

From each of 50 assorted brown print nickels, cut:
- 4 squares, 2½" x 2½" (200 total)

Refer to the cutting diagram.

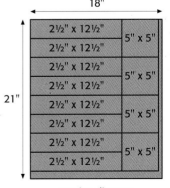

Cutting diagram for brown fat quarters   Cutting diagram for blue fat quarters

Pieced by Claudia Plett; designed and machine quilted by Le Ann Weaver

From *each* of 20 assorted brown print nickels, cut:
- 4 squares, 2" x 2" (80 total)

From *each* of 40 assorted blue print nickels, cut:
- 4 squares, 2½" x 2½" (160 total)

From *each* of 40 assorted blue print nickels, cut:
- 2 rectangles, 2" x 5" (80 total)

From *each* of the 3 remaining assorted blue print nickels, cut:
- 4 squares, 2½" x 2½" (12 total)

From the brown print fabric for inner border, corner squares, and binding, cut:
- 7 strips, 2½" x 42"
- 4 squares, 5½" x 5½"
- 8 strips, 2¼" x 42"

Making the Blocks

1. Referring to "Half-Square-Triangle Units" on page 85, draw a diagonal line on the wrong side of each cream 2½" square and on 80 of the blue 2½" squares. Combine cream, brown, and blue squares to make half-square-triangle units as shown. Press the seam allowances toward the darker prints. Trim the units to measure 2" x 2".

Make 240.   Make 160.   Make 160.

TRIM AND TREAT

When you have a lot of half-square-triangle units to trim, invite friends or your stitching group to get together and have a trimming tea party! Have plenty of rotary cutters and mats available—along with cookies, of course!

---

2. Using the brown 2" squares, cream 2" x 3½" rectangles, cream 2" x 5" rectangles, blue 2" x 5" rectangles, and the half-square-triangle units from step 1, make quarter-block units as shown. Make sure to rotate the half-square-triangle

units into the correct position. Press the seam allowances as indicated. The units should measure 6½" x 6½".

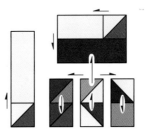

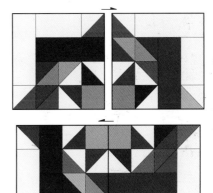

Make 80.

3. Combine the units from step 2 as shown. Your blocks should each measure 12½" x 12½". Make 20 blocks.

Make 20.

Assembling the Quilt Top

1. Join four blocks and three brown 2½" x 12½" strips into a row. Press the seam allowances toward the strips. Make five rows.

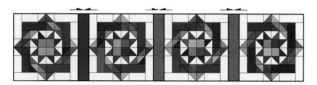

Make 5.

2. Use the remaining brown 2½" x 12½" strips and blue 2½" squares to make four sashing rows as shown. Press the seam allowances toward the strips.

Make 4.

3. Matching the seam intersections, sew the block rows and sashing rows together to form the quilt center. Press the seam allowances toward the sashing.

Adding the Borders

1. Stitch the brown 2½"-wide strips together end to end. Referring to "Borders with Butted Corners" on page 91, measure and cut the strips, and sew them to the sides and then to the top and bottom of the quilt top for the inner border. Press the seam allowances toward the border strips.

2. Sew the 18 blue rectangles together end to end for the outer border. Press the seam allowances open. Measure your quilt through the center both ways and cut two side border strips and two top and bottom border strips to the correct measurements.

3. Stitch the side borders to the left and right edges of your quilt top. Press the seam allowances toward the outer border.

4. Add the brown 5½" squares to the ends of the top and bottom borders. Stitch the strips to your quilt top. Press toward the outer border.

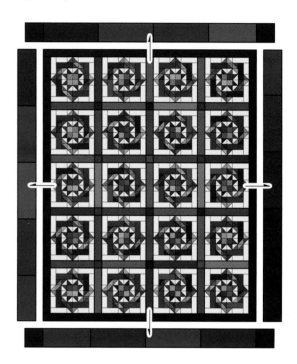

Finishing the Quilt

Refer to "Finishing" on page 93 for detailed instructions, if needed.

1. Piece the quilt backing so that it is 4" to 6" longer and wider than the quilt top.

2. Layer the quilt top with backing and batting. Baste with thread for hand quilting or with safety pins for machine quilting. If you're taking your quilt to a long-arm quilter, you do not need to layer and baste it.

3. Hand or machine quilt as desired.

4. Trim the batting and backing so that the edges are even with the quilt top. Use the brown 2¼"-wide strips to bind the edges of the quilt.

Luck of the Irish

Υou don't have to be Irish to gather lots of greens for this scrappy Nine Patch quilt. Evelyn found a happy home for many of her smaller scraps in this lucky quilt.

Finished quilt size: 51" x 75"
Finished block size: 9" x 9"

Materials

Yardage is based on 42"-wide fabric. Fat eighths measure 9" x 21".

2⅛ yards of dark green background print for blocks, sashing, and border

1½ to 2 yards *total, or* 12 to 16 fat eighths, of assorted medium to dark green prints for blocks

1½ to 1¾ yards *total, or* 12 to 14 fat eighths, of assorted light prints for blocks

1⅜ yards of light green background print for blocks and sashing

⅝ yard of fabric for binding

3⅛ yards of fabric for backing

57" x 81" piece of batting

Cutting

From the assorted medium to dark green prints, cut a total of*:
- 60 strips, 1½" x 21"

From the assorted light prints, cut a total of*:
- 46 strips, 1½" x 21"

From the light green background print, cut:
- 7 strips, 4" x 42"; crosscut into 67 squares, 4" x 4"
- 4 strips, 3½" x 42"; crosscut into 38 squares, 3½" x 3½"

From the dark green background print, cut:
- 7 strips, 4" x 42"; crosscut into 67 squares, 4" x 4"
- 11 strips, 3½" x 42"; crosscut *4 of the strips* into 38 squares, 3½" x 3½". Save the rest of the strips for the border.

From the binding fabric, cut:
- 7 strips, 2½" x 42"

*If you're using scraps, cut strips 1½" by whatever lengths you have.

Making the Blocks

1. From the 1½"-wide strips of assorted medium green, dark green, and light fabrics, choose a medium or dark fabric and a light fabric for a nine-patch unit. From the dark fabric, cut two pieces, 1½" x 10", and one piece, 1½" x 5". From the light fabric, cut one piece, 1½" x 10", and two pieces, 1½" x 5".

2. Make a strip set with the two 1½" x 10" lengths of dark green and one 1½" x 10" length of light print. Make a second strip set with the 5" lengths, using two lights and one dark as shown. Crosscut the 10" strip set into six segments, 1½" wide, and crosscut the 5" strip set into three segments, 1½" wide.

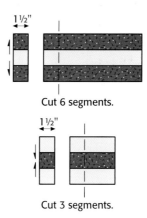

Cut 6 segments.

Cut 3 segments.

Made by Evelyn Sloppy

3. Assemble the nine-patch units. Each pair of strip sets will make three blocks. Repeat to make a total of 135 nine-patch units. They should measure 3½" x 3½".

Make 135.

4. Referring to "Half-Square-Triangle Units" on page 85, draw a diagonal line on the wrong side of each 4" light green square, and layer the squares with the 4" dark green squares to make 134 half-square-triangle units. Trim the units to measure 3½" x 3½".

Make 134.

5. Sew five assorted nine-patch units and four half-square-triangle units together to make a block as shown. Repeat to make a total of 24 blocks. Blocks should measure 9½" x 9½".

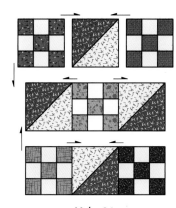

Make 24.

Making the Sashing Units

Sew the remaining half-square-triangle units and the 3½" light green and dark green squares together to make the sashing units. Make 38 units.

Make 38.

Assembling the Quilt Top

1. Lay out four blocks and three sashing units in a row as shown. Join the pieces and press the seam allowances toward the sashing units. Make a total of six block rows.

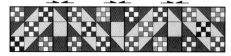

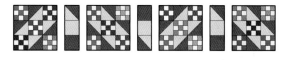

Make 6 rows.

2. Lay out four sashing units and three nine-patch units in a row as shown. Join the pieces and press the seam allowances toward the sashing units. Make three of sashing row 1.

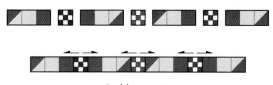

Sashing row 1.
Make 3.

3. Repeat step 2 to make two of sashing row 2.

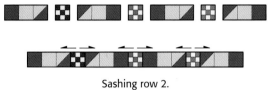

Sashing row 2.
Make 2.

4. Lay out the block rows and the sashing rows as shown. Join the rows. Press the seam allowances toward the sashing rows.

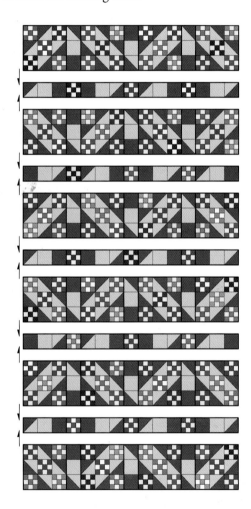

5. Sew the dark green 3½"-wide strips together end to end. Referring to "Borders with Butted Corners" on page 91, measure and cut the strips, and sew them to the sides and then to the top and bottom of the quilt top for the outer border.

Finishing the Quilt

Refer to "Finishing" on page 93 for detailed instructions, if needed.

1. Piece the quilt backing so that it is 4" to 6" longer and wider than the quilt top.

2. Layer the quilt top with backing and batting. Baste with thread for hand quilting or with safety pins for machine quilting. If you're taking your quilt to a long-arm quilter, you do not need to layer and baste it.

3. Hand or machine quilt as desired.

4. Trim the batting and backing so that the edges are even with the quilt top. Use the 2½"-wide binding strips to bind the edges of the quilt.

Double Windmill

When published in the *Spokane Daily Chronicle* newspaper, Alice Brooks' Depression-era "Double Windmill" pattern was described as "simple." It is an easy quilt with only two pattern pieces, but it has the potential to be a showcase for a large collection of prints, feeding the eye of an appreciative viewer. In the dust-bowl years of the Depression, the windmills were especially important to pump much-needed water and offered a companionable sound to remote farmhouses. Hand-quilted swirls of wind bring Karen's windmills to life.

Finished quilt size: 83" x 94"
Finished block size: 11" x 11"

Materials

Yardage is based on 42"-wide fabric.
6½ yards of unbleached muslin for blocks and borders
4 yards *total* of assorted 1930s reproduction prints for blocks and outer border
¾ yard of yellow print for binding
3 yards of 90"-wide unbleached muslin for backing*
89" x 100" piece of batting
Template plastic
If using 42"-wide unbleached muslin, you'll need 8¼ yards (3 widths pieced horizontally).

Cutting

Template pattern for piece A appears on page 33. For detailed instructions, refer to "Making Templates" on page 87.

From the assorted 1930s reproduction prints, cut *a total of*:
- 146 squares, 3⅝" x 3⅝"; cut each square in half diagonally to yield 292 triangles
- 168 pieces with template A

From the *lengthwise grain* of the unbleached muslin, cut:
- 2 strips, 6" x 92"
- 2 strips, 6" x 70"

From the remaining unbleached muslin, cut:
- 21 strips, 3¼" x 42"; cut into 168 pieces with template A*
- 146 squares, 3⅝" x 3⅝"; cut each square in half diagonally to yield 292 triangles

From the yellow print, cut:
- 10 strips, 2¼" x 42"

If you're using muslin or a solid fabric, you don't need to cut reverse pieces; however, if you substitute a fabric that has a right side and a wrong side, cut 168 pieces with template A reversed.

Pieced and quilted by Karen Earlywine

Making the Blocks

1. Sew each muslin half-square triangle to a print A piece as shown. Press the seam allowances toward the A piece. Sew each print half-square triangle to a muslin A piece. Press the seam allowances toward the print triangle. Refer to "Chain Piecing" on page 85 to make the sewing process quicker, if desired. Make 168 of each unit.

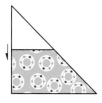
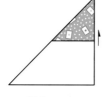

Make 168.   Make 168.

2. In a pleasing mix of colors, arrange eight units as shown. Pin and sew two units together along the long edges, matching the seams, to make a square unit. Be careful not to stretch the bias edges as you stitch. Press the seam allowances toward the print A piece. Make four square units for each block (168 total).

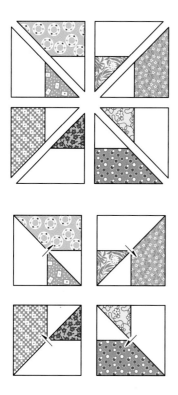

3. Using a ruler, trim each square unit to measure 6" x 6" by placing the 45° line on your ruler along the diagonal seam. Be sure to trim off the dog-ears.

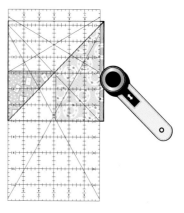

4. Sew the square units together in pairs to make a half block. Sew two half blocks together, matching the seams, to complete the block. Make a total of 42 blocks. Trim them to 11½" x 11½", referring to "Squaring Up Blocks" on page 91 as needed.

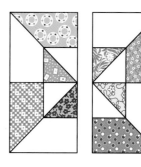

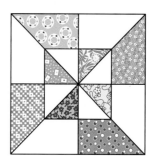

Make 42.

Assembling the Quilt Top

1. Arrange the blocks in seven rows of six blocks each as shown in the quilt assembly diagram. Rearrange the blocks until you're pleased with the color placement.

2. Sew the blocks into rows. Press the seam allowances in alternate directions from row to row. Stitch the rows together. Press the seam allowances in one direction.

3. Refer to "Borders with Butted Corners" on page 91. Using the muslin 6"-wide strips, measure and cut the shorter strips, and sew them to the top and bottom of the quilt top. Repeat to add the longer strips to the sides of the quilt top. Press all seam allowances toward the newly added borders. The quilt top should measure 77½" x 88½" for the outer border to fit properly.

4. Sew the remaining print half-square triangles and muslin half-square triangles together along their long edges to make 124 half-square-triangle units. Press the seam allowances toward the print triangles.

5. Sew 30 half-square-triangle units together for the top border. Be sure all the print triangles are facing in the direction shown in the assembly diagram. Repeat to make the bottom border.

6. Sew 32 half-square-triangle units together in the same manner for each side border. Make two side-border strips.

7. Referring to the quilt assembly diagram, pin and sew the side-border strips to the right and left edges of the quilt top. Press the seam allowances toward the muslin strips.

8. Sew the border strips from step 5 to the top and bottom of the quilt top. Press the seam allowances toward the muslin strips.

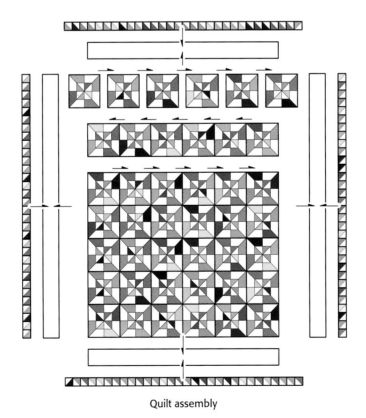

Quilt assembly

Finishing the Quilt

Refer to "Finishing" on page 93 for detailed instructions, if needed.

1. Piece the quilt backing so that it is 4" to 6" longer and wider than the quilt top.

2. Mark the quilting lines using a swirl design or your own favorite quilting design.

3. Layer the quilt top with backing and batting. Baste with thread for hand quilting or with safety pins for machine quilting. If you're taking your quilt to a long-arm quilter, you do not need to layer and baste it.

4. Hand or machine quilt as desired. The quilt shown is hand quilted following the marked lines and stitched in the ditch around all of the print pieces.

5. Trim the batting and backing so that the edges are even with the quilt top. Use the yellow 2¼"-wide strips to bind the edges of the quilt.

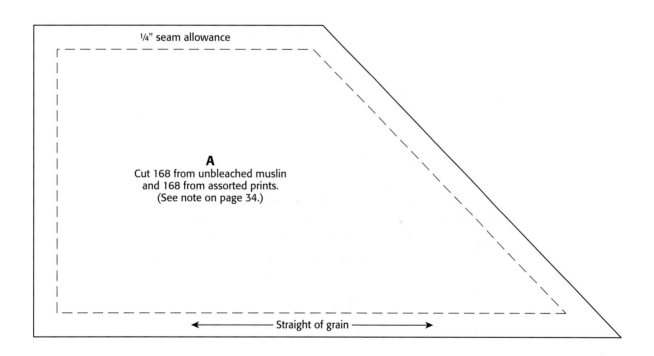

¼" seam allowance

A
Cut 168 from unbleached muslin and 168 from assorted prints. (See note on page 34.)

◄──────── Straight of grain ────────►

Pieced by Judy Dafoe Hopkins; quilted by Barbara Ford

Arctic Nights

In positive-negative (or "counterchange") designs, the light and dark areas reverse from block to block (or from quadrant to quadrant within the block, as in the quilt shown). Positive-negative designs always work well for scrappy-looking quilts, and they're an excellent choice for two-fabric quilts as well. For example, the Arctic Nights block would be terrific made up in muslin and a red solid, or using a single light print and a single dark print.

Finished quilt size: 60" x 76"
Finished block size: 8" x 8"

Materials

Yardage is based on 42"-wide fabric.
⅛ yard *each* of 32 assorted light prints for blocks*
⅛ yard *each* of 32 assorted dark blue, bluish green, and green prints for blocks*
¼ yard *each* of 7 assorted light prints for border
¾ yard of green print for binding
5 yards of fabric for backing
66" x 82" piece of batting
If you wish to use the same fabric more than once, you can purchase ⅜ yard each of 8 assorted light prints and cut 4 strips, 2½" x 42", from each one.

Cutting

From *each* of the assorted light prints for blocks, cut:
- 1 strip, 2½" x 42" (32 total)

From *each* of the assorted dark prints for blocks, cut:
- 1 strip, 2½" x 42" (32 total)

From *each* of the assorted light prints for border, cut:
- 1 strip, 6½" x 42" (7 total); crosscut the strips into a total of:
    - 17 rectangles, 6½" x 12½" (A)
    - 3 rectangles, 6½" x 10½" (B)
    - 1 rectangle, 6½" x 14½" (C)

From the green print for binding, cut:
- 8 strips, 2½" x 42"

Making the Blocks

This is one of those designs that creates an occasional pressing conundrum no matter what you do. If you press the seam allowances open, you may have difficulty matching seams, and you'll have no "ditch" to stitch in when you reach the quilting stage. If you press to the side, you may have to twist some seam allowances on the back when you assemble the blocks and/or the quilt, to make them butt together properly for easy joining.

1. Layer a 2½"-wide light strip with a 2½"-wide dark strip, right sides together and long edges aligned. Square up one end of this layered strip pair, then cut: three rectangles, 2½" x 4½" (A), three squares, 2½" x 2½" (B), and three rectangles, 1½" x 2½" (C). Set these pieces aside for now.

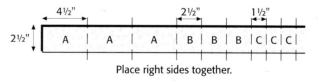

Place right sides together.

2. From the remaining piece of the layered strip pair, cut one strip, 1½" by about 11", as shown.

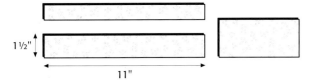

3. Join the 1½" x 11" layered strips along one long edge to make a strip unit. Press the seam allowances open or toward the darker fabric. The strip unit should measure 2½" wide (raw edge to raw edge) when sewn. From this strip unit, cut a total of six segments, 1½" wide.

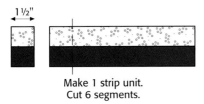

Make 1 strip unit.
Cut 6 segments.

4. Join a segment from step 3 to each of the C rectangles from step 1 as shown, being careful to orient the segments in the correct direction in each combination. Make three of each combination. Press the seam allowances open or in the direction indicated. The units should measure 2½" x 2½".

Make 3.   Make 3.

5. Join the B squares from step 1 to the units from step 4 as shown, being careful to add the correct light or dark square to the unit indicated. Make three of each combination. Press the seam allowances open or in the direction indicated. The units should measure 2½" x 4½".

Make 3.   Make 3.

6. Stitch the A rectangles from step 1 to the units from step 5 as shown, being careful to add the correct light or dark rectangle to the unit indicated. Make three dark units and three light units. Press the seam allowances open or in the direction indicated. The units should measure 4½" x 4½".

Dark unit.   Light unit.
Make 3.   Make 3.

7. Repeat steps 1–6 with the remaining 2½"-wide light strips and dark strips. You can work with several layered strip pairs at once if you wish. Just remember that each finished unit should contain just two fabrics—one light and one dark. When you have cut and stitched all 32 sets of strips, you'll have 96 light units and 96 dark units (192 total).

8. Randomly join two light units and two dark units to make 48 blocks as shown. Press the seam allowances however you wish. The blocks should measure 8½" x 8½".

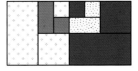

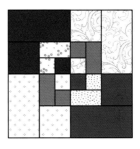

Make 48.

Assembling the Quilt Top

1. Join the blocks to make eight rows of six blocks each as shown below. Note that the blocks should be arranged so that blue, bluish green, or green corners appear at the upper left and lower right. Press the seam allowances in opposite directions from row to row. Join the rows. Press the seam allowances in one direction.

2. Join the border pieces end to end to make four pieced border strips as shown. Attach the border strips to the bottom edge of the quilt, then the sides, and finally the top edge. Press the seam allowances toward the just-added border strip.

Finishing the Quilt

Refer to "Finishing" on page 93 for detailed instructions, if needed.

1. Piece the quilt backing so that it is 4" to 6" longer and wider than the quilt top.

2. Layer the quilt top with backing and batting. Baste with thread for hand quilting or with safety pins for machine quilting. If you're taking your quilt to a long-arm quilter, you do not need to layer and baste it.

3. Hand or machine quilt as desired.

4. Trim the batting and backing so that the edges are even with the quilt top. Use the 2½"-wide green strips to bind the edges of the quilt.

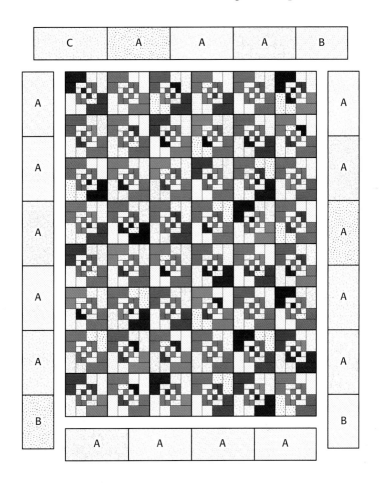

Made by Pat Speth

Buffalo Ridge

$\mathcal{A}$ large assortment of plaids and prints set against a tan-and-plaid background make this a visually active quilt. Tone-on-tone prints were used for the strips in the block centers and look like solids from a distance.

Finished quilt size: 78½" x 94½"
Finished block size: 14" x 14"

Materials

Yardage is based on 42"-wide fabric.
116 squares, 5" x 5", of assorted prints for blocks and pieced border
116 squares, 5" x 5", of assorted plaids for blocks and pieced border
2½ yards of light background print for blocks and pieced border
⅛ yard *each* of 20 assorted tone-on-tone prints for blocks
¾ yard of dark print for inner border
2⅓ yards of medium print for outer border and binding
7½ yards of fabric for backing
85" x 101" piece of batting

Cutting

From the light background print, cut:
- 12 strips, 2⅞" x 42"; crosscut into 160 squares, 2⅞" x 2⅞". Cut each square in half diagonally to yield 320 triangles.
- 20 strips, 2½" x 42"; crosscut into 308 squares, 2½" x 2½"

From the *each* of the assorted tone-on-tone prints, cut:
- 1 strip, 2½" x 42"; crosscut into 4 rectangles, 2½" x 6½" (80 total, keeping like prints together)

From the dark print, cut:
- 3 strips, 3½" x 42"
- 4 strips, 2½" x 42"

From the medium print, cut:
- 9 strips, 5½" x 42"
- 10 strips, 2½" x 42"

Making the Blocks

For each block you'll need:
- 4 assorted print squares, 5" x 5"
- 16 background half-square triangles
- 4 assorted plaid squares, 5" x 5"
- 4 matching tone-on-tone print rectangles, 2½" x 6½"
- 1 background square, 2½" x 2½"

1. Cut each 5" print square into four squares, 2½" x 2½". You'll use only three of the smaller squares; set aside the remaining smaller squares to use in another project. Arrange each set of three matching squares with four of the background half-square triangles in horizontal rows as shown. Sew the pieces together and press the seam allowances toward the squares. Sew the rows together and press as directed.

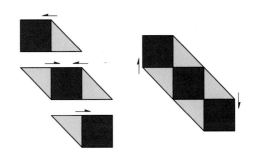

2. Trim the four 5" plaid squares to measure 4⅞" x 4⅞". Cut each square in half diagonally to yield two triangles. Sew the plaid half-square triangles to the units from step 1. Make four of these units.

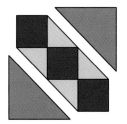 

Make 4
for each block.

3. Arrange the four units from step 2, four matching tone-on-tone rectangles, and one 2½" background square in horizontal rows. Sew the pieces together in rows and press the seam allowances toward the tone-on-tone rectangles. Sew the rows together to complete the Buffalo Ridge block.

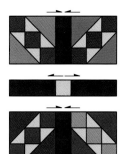

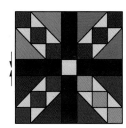

Buffalo Ridge block

4. Repeat steps 1–3 to make 20 blocks.

Making the Pieced Border

1. Using the remaining 5" assorted plaid and print squares, trim each square ½" from one edge. Then cut the trimmed piece in half in the opposite direction from the first cut so that the two resulting pieces each measure 2½" x 4½".

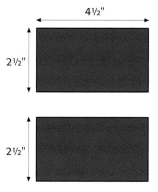

Trim ½" from one edge.

Make 288.

2. Refer to "Flying-Geese Units" on page 86. Draw a diagonal line on the wrong side of each remaining 2½" background square. Use the marked squares and the rectangles from step 1 to make 288 flying-geese units.

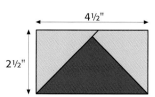

3. Sew the units together in pairs to make 144 border blocks.

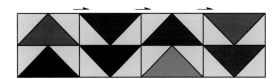

Flying-geese border block

4. Arrange and sew 19 blocks together, alternating the direction of the points along the length of the strip for each side border. Press the seam allowances in one direction. Make two side-border strips.

5. In the same manner, arrange and sew 17 blocks together for the top border. Repeat to make the bottom border.

Assembling the Quilt Top

1. Referring to the quilt plan at right and working on your design wall, arrange the blocks in five rows of four blocks each. Sew the blocks together in rows and press the seam allowances in opposite directions from row to row.

2. Sew the rows together and press the seam allowances in one direction.

3. Sew the 2½"-wide dark print strips together end to end. Referring to "Borders with Butted Corners" on page 91, measure and cut the strips, and sew them to the sides of the quilt top for the inner border. Repeat with the 3½"-wide strips to add the top and bottom borders to the quilt top.

4. Sew the 19-unit pieced border strips to the sides of the quilt top. Sew the 17-unit pieced border strips to the top and bottom of the quilt top. Press all seam allowances toward the inner border.

5. Sew the 5½"-wide medium print strips together end to end. Measure and cut the strips, and sew them to the sides and then to the top and bottom of the quilt top for the outer border. Refer to "Borders with Butted Corners" as needed.

Finishing the Quilt

Refer to "Finishing" on page 93 for detailed instructions, if needed.

1. Piece the quilt backing so that it is 4" to 6" longer and wider than the quilt top.

2. Layer the quilt top with backing and batting. Baste with thread for hand quilting or with safety pins for machine quilting. If you're taking your quilt to a long-arm quilter, you do not need to layer and baste it.

3. Hand or machine quilt as desired.

4. Trim the batting and backing so that the edges are even with the quilt top. Use the 2½"-wide medium print strips to bind the edges of the quilt.

Designed by Mimi Dietrich; pieced and appliquéd by the Vintage Quilters: Shelly Cornwell,
Karan Flanscha, Nancy Hayes, Barbara Jacobson, Sharri Nottger, and Robin Venter;
machine quilted by Joyce Kuehl

Vintage Memories

Take your guests on a trip into the past with a collection of new fabrics that look vintage. The scrappy reproduction prints include colors from the heritage of American quilts—indigo blue, Turkey red, cheddar gold, and double pink. A touch of appliqué across the pillow area and border adds vines, leaves, flowers, birds, berries, and pineapples, a symbol of colonial hospitality. Whether this quilt tops an antique bed carved with pineapples or something a little more modern, it will welcome your guests with a feeling of tradition and comfort.

Finished quilt size: 91⅝" x 100½"
Finished block size: 4" x 4"

Materials

Yardage is based on 42"-wide fabric.

6½ yards of tan print for setting blocks, triangles, and outer border

5 yards *total* of assorted reproduction prints, including golds, blues, reds, pinks, yellows, purples, blacks, and greens for blocks and appliqués

1½ yards of dark green print for appliquéd vines and binding

½ yard of plum print for inner border

8⅝ yards of fabric for backing

98" x 107" piece of batting

Cutting

Patterns for the flowers, leaves, berries, birds, and pineapple are on pages 46–48.

From the assorted reproduction prints, cut:
- 190 squares, 5" x 5"; cut each square into 4 squares, 2½" x 2½" (760 total squares; 380 pairs)

Cut the remaining assorted reproduction prints as follows:

From a gold print, cut:
- 3 pineapples

From a blue print, cut:
- 6 birds
- 6 bird wings

From a pink print, cut:
- 12 flowers

From a yellow print, cut:
- 12 flower centers

From a purple print, cut:
- 54 berries

From the assorted green prints, cut:
- 73 leaves

From the *lengthwise grain* of the tan print, cut:
- 2 strips, 8½" x 104"
- 1 strip, 8½" x 95"

From the remaining tan print, cut:
- 23 strips, 4½" x 42"; crosscut strips into 180 squares, 4½" x 4½"
- 14 squares, 6⅞" x 6⅞"; cut each square twice diagonally to make 56 side setting triangles (2 are extra)
- 2 squares, 3¾" x 3¾"; cut each square in half diagonally to make 4 corner setting triangles

From the plum print, cut:
- 10 strips, 1½" x 42"

From the dark green print, cut:
- 10 binding strips, 2" x 42"
- ⅝"-wide bias strips (8 yards total length)

Making the Four Patch Blocks

You need 190 Four Patch blocks for this quilt.

1. Separate the 2½" squares into 380 matching pairs. Arrange two pairs to make each block.

2. Sew two squares together, and then join the pairs to make a Four Patch block. Repeat to make 190 Four Patch blocks.

Four Patch block
Make 190.

Assembling the Quilt Top

1. Arrange the Four Patch blocks and 4½" tan squares and setting triangles in rows as shown. Lay the blocks out on a floor or design wall to help you distribute the colors evenly. You should have 13 vertical rows of Four Patch blocks set on point, with 16 blocks in each row (except in the "pillow" area).

2. Referring to the illustration above, sew the blocks together into three large units. This assembly will make it easier for you to appliqué the pillow design before sewing the entire quilt together.

3. Photocopy the appliqué border patterns A, B, and C on pages 46–48 and tape them together using the pillow panel vine line. Trace the pineapple in the center of the pillow panel; then trace the vines on either side. Use a light box to trace the design in reverse on the left side of the pineapple.

4. Fold the long edges of the ⅝" dark green bias strips into the center of the strips, wrong sides together so that the raw edges meet. Baste along the edges with small stitches to make the vines. Gently pull on one of the basting threads to ease the bias strip into a curved shape.

Pull thread to create curve.

5. Appliqué the vines, leaves, flowers, berries, and birds using your favorite appliqué techniques.

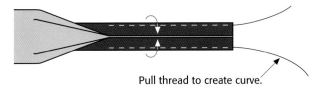

Pillow-tuck appliqué placement

6. When the appliqué is complete, sew the three units together to complete the quilt center.

Adding the Borders

1. Sew the plum print border strips together end to end. From the long strip, cut one 75⅝"-long strip and sew it to the top of the quilt. Cut one 95"-long strip and sew it to the long edge of the 95"-long tan strip. Cut two 104"-long strips and sew them to the long edges of the 104"-long tan strips.

2. Matching the plum edges of the borders to the top of the quilt, sew the 104"-long side borders to the edges of the quilt, stopping ¼" from the bottom corner. Make sure the plum borders are attached to the quilt top, not the tan ones.

3. Sew the 95"-long border to the bottom of the quilt, again making sure the plum border is attached to the quilt top. Stop sewing ¼" from the corners.

4. Miter the two bottom quilt corners, referring to "Borders with Mitered Corners" on page 92.

5. Photocopy the appliqué border patterns A, B, and C (pages 46–48) and tape them together using the border vine line.

6. Trace the pineapple in the center of the mitered corner; then trace the vines on either side. Use a light box to trace the design in reverse on the left side of the pineapple.

7. Appliqué the vines, leaves, flowers, berries, and birds using your favorite appliqué techniques.

Border appliqué placement

Finishing the Quilt

Refer to "Finishing" on page 93 for detailed instructions, if needed.

1. Piece the quilt backing so that it is 4" to 6" longer and wider than the quilt top.

2. Layer the quilt top with backing and batting. Baste with thread for hand quilting or with safety pins for machine quilting. If you're taking your quilt to a long-arm quilter, you do not need to layer and baste it.

3. Hand or machine quilt as desired.

4. Trim the batting and backing so that the edges are even with the quilt top. Use the 2"-wide dark green strips to bind the edges of the quilt.

Match to pillow center.

Mitered border

Border vine

Pillow panel vine

Match to appliqué pattern B on page 47.

Appliqué pattern A
Patterns do not include
seam allowances.

Match to appliqué pattern C on page 48.

Appliqué pattern B
Patterns do not include
seam allowances.

Match to appliqué pattern A on page 46.

Appliqué pattern C
Patterns do not include
seam allowances.

Match to appliqué pattern B on page 47.

Confetti

Nancy's passion for batik fabrics has resulted in an extensive stash, which provided ample inspiration as she was designing this quilt. The important component is the contrast between the very light and very dark fabrics to create movement and hidden stars.

Finished quilt size: 52¾" x 62¾"
Finished block size: 5" x 5"

Materials

Yardage is based on 42"-wide fabric.

2¾ yards *total* of assorted light batiks for blocks

2¾ yards *total* of assorted dark batiks for blocks

¼ yard of yellow batik for inner border

1⅝ yards of multicolored batik for outer border

½ yard of fabric for binding

3⅜ yards of fabric for backing

59" x 69" piece of batting

Cutting

From the assorted light batiks, cut *a total of*:
- 50 squares, 2¼" x 2¼"
- 98 squares, 2" x 2"; cut each square in half diagonally to yield 196 triangles
- 100 squares, 2½" x 2½"; cut each square in half diagonally to yield 200 triangles
- 98 squares, 3¼" x 3¼"; cut each square in half diagonally to yield 196 triangles

From the assorted dark batiks, cut *a total of*:
- 49 squares, 2¼" x 2¼"
- 100 squares, 2" x 2"; cut each square in half diagonally to yield 200 triangles
- 98 squares, 2½" x 2½"; cut each square in half diagonally to yield 196 triangles
- 100 squares, 3¼" x 3¼"; cut each square in half diagonally to yield 200 triangles

From the yellow batik, cut:
- 5 strips, 1⅛" x 42"

From the *lengthwise grain* of the multicolored batik, cut:
- 2 strips, 3½" x 58"
- 2 strips, 3½" x 54"

From the binding fabric, cut:
- 7 strips, 2" x 42"

Making the Blocks

1. Refer to "Paper Foundation Piecing" on page 86. Make 99 copies of the Square-on-Square foundation pattern on page 52.

2. For block A, place a dark square, right side up, on the *wrong* side of the foundation, covering area 1. Position a 2" light triangle, right side down, with the long raw edge aligned with the edge of the dark square so that it extends approximately ¼" over the line between areas 1 and 2. Sew on the line between areas 1 and 2, starting ¼" before the line and extending ¼" beyond.

3. Fold the paper back to reveal the seam allowance. Trim the seam allowance to ¼", and then press it to one side. Continue adding matching 2" light triangles for pieces 3, 4, and 5. Remember to trim the seam allowances as needed and press the pieces open after each addition.

Made by Nancy Mahoney; machine quilted by Barbara Ford

4. Repeat the process to add matching 2½" dark triangles for pieces 6, 7, 8, and 9. Then add 3¼" matching light triangles for pieces 10, 11, 12, and 13. Make 49 of block A.

Block A.
Make 49.

5. For block B, repeat steps 2, 3, and 4 using a light square for piece 1 and matching 2" dark triangles for pieces 2, 3, 4, and 5. Then add matching 2½" light triangles for pieces 6, 7, 8, and 9. Finally, add matching 3¼" dark triangles for pieces 10, 11, 12, and 13. Make 50 of block B.

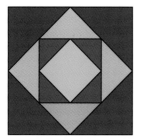

Block B.
Make 50.

6. Trim the fabric extending around the edge of the foundation paper so that there is a ¼" seam allowance around each block. Carefully remove the foundation paper.

Assembling the Quilt Top

1. On a design wall, lay out the blocks in 11 rows of nine blocks each, alternating blocks A and B in each row. When you're pleased with the arrangement, sew the blocks together into rows. Press the seam allowances in opposite directions from row to row. Sew the rows

together and press the seam allowances in one direction.

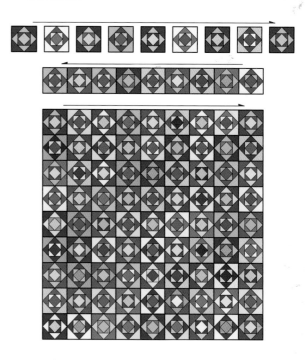

2. Sew the yellow 1⅛"-wide strips together end to end. Referring to "Borders with Butted Corners" on pages 91, measure and cut the strips, and sew them to the sides and then to the top and bottom of the quilt top for the inner border.

3. Measure and cut the multicolored 3½"-wide strips, and sew them to the quilt top for the outer border.

Finishing the Quilt

Refer to "Finishing" on page 93 for detailed instructions, if needed.

1. Piece the quilt backing so that it is 4" to 6" longer and wider than the quilt top.

2. Layer the quilt top with backing and batting. Baste with thread for hand quilting or with safety pins for machine quilting. If you're taking your quilt to a long-arm quilter, you do not need to layer and baste it.

3. Hand or machine quilt as desired.

4. Trim the batting and backing so that the edges are even with the quilt top. Use the 2"-wide binding strips to bind the edges of the quilt.

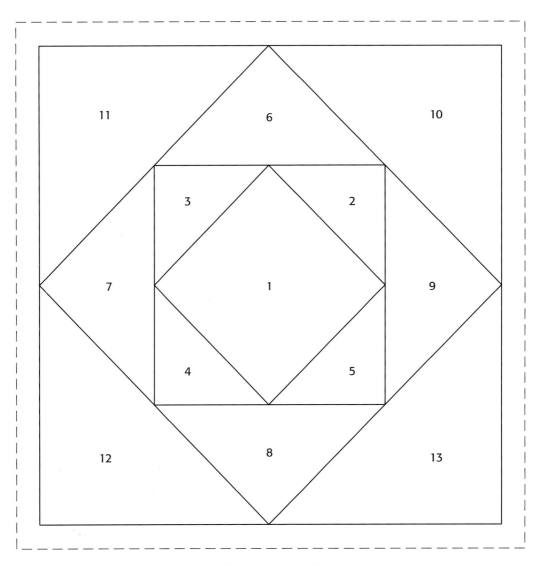

Square-on-Square foundation pattern

Lattice Make a Quilt

This quilt includes both a diagonal and a horizontal grid pattern. The two grids result from careful value placement. Choose very light fabrics along with a medium fabric for the four-patch units and a very dark fabric for what appears to be lattice forming the diagonal grid. Red is a strong color that works well as the accent.

Finished quilt size: 70" x 70"
Finished block size: 9" x 9"

Materials

Yardage is based on 42"-wide fabric.

2¼ yards of black-and-gray floral for outer border

⅞ yard of gray floral for alternate blocks

⅞ yard of light gray tone-on-tone fabric for setting triangles and inner border

⅞ yard of black-and-gray polka-dot fabric for lattice

½ yard of red fabric for cornerstones and middle border

16 strips, 2½" x 21", of assorted medium fabrics for four-patch units

16 strips, 2½" x 21", of assorted light fabrics for four-patch units

⅔ yard of medium gray fabric for binding

4¾ yards of fabric for backing

76" x 76" piece of batting

Cutting

From the black-and-gray polka-dot fabric, cut:
- 5 strips, 4½" x 42"; crosscut into 128 rectangles, 1½" x 4½"

From the red fabric, cut:
- 8 strips, 1½" x 42"; crosscut *2 of the strips* into 41 squares, 1½" x 1½".

From the gray floral, cut:
- 6 strips, 4½" x 42"; crosscut into 48 squares, 4½" x 4½"

From the light gray tone-on-tone fabric, cut:
- 2 strips, 9" x 42"; crosscut into 8 squares, 9" x 9". Cut each square twice diagonally to yield 32 setting triangles.
- 6 strips, 1½" x 42"
- 4 rectangles, 1½" x 2"

From the *lengthwise grain* of the black-and-gray floral, cut:
- 2 strips, 7" x 74"
- 2 strips, 7" x 64"

From the medium gray fabric, cut:
- 8 strips, 2½" x 42"

Making the Four-Patch Unit Blocks

1. Sew a polka-dot rectangle to each side of a red square; press toward the polka-dot fabric. Make 16.

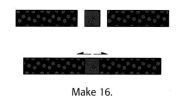

Make 16.

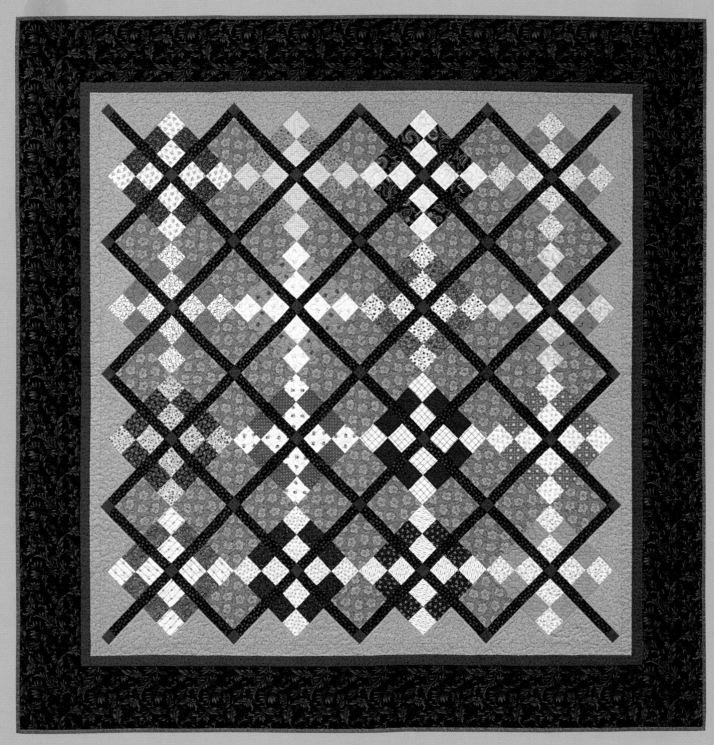

Made by Lynn Roddy Brown

2. To make four-patch units, join a light 2½" x 21" strip to a medium 2½" x 21" strip along their long edges; press the seam allowances toward the medium fabric. Cut the strip set into eight 2½" segments.

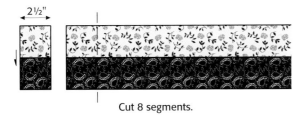

Cut 8 segments.

3. Place two segments right sides together with seams butting. Use straight pins to secure the seams. Sew the pair together as shown. Press the seam allowances open. Make four four-patch units.

Make 4.

4. Arrange the four-patch units, a pieced unit from step 1, and two polka-dot rectangles as shown. Join four-patch units to each side of the polka-dot rectangles, making certain the four-patch units are in the correct position. Press the seam allowances toward the rectangles. Join the rows, carefully matching the seam intersections. Press the seam allowances toward the center.

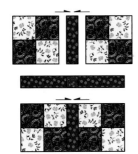

5. Repeat steps 2–4 to make a total of 16 blocks.

Making the Alternate Blocks

1. Join a polka-dot rectangle to each side of a red square. Press toward the red square. Make nine.

2. Arrange four gray floral squares, a pieced unit from step 1, and two polka-dot rectangles as shown. Join the gray floral squares to the polka-dot rectangles. Press the seam allowances toward the gray floral. Join the rows, carefully matching the seam intersections. Press the seam allowances toward the gray floral.

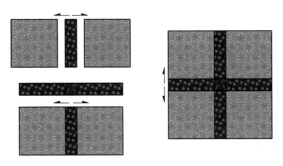

3. Repeat step 2 to make a total of nine alternate blocks.

Making the Setting Triangles

1. To make the side setting triangles, sew a polka-dot rectangle to one side of a gray floral square. Press the seam allowances toward the gray floral.

2. Sew a red square to the end of a polka-dot rectangle; press the seam allowances toward the red square. Sew the pieced strip to an adjacent side of the unit from step 1. Press the seam allowances toward the gray floral.

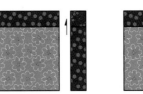

3. Align a gray tone-on-tone setting triangle with the unit from step 2 so that the right-angle corner of the triangle aligns with the polka-dot corner. Starting at the corner, sew the pieces together along the polka-dot edge. Press the seam allowances toward the setting triangle and trim the point as shown.

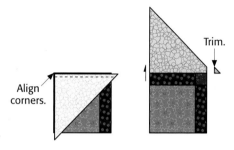

4. Add a second setting triangle, aligning the right-angle corner of the triangle with the remaining polka-dot corner. Starting at the corner, sew the pieces together and press the seam allowances toward the setting triangle.

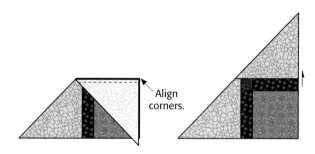

5. Repeat steps 1–4 to make a total of 12 side setting triangles.

6. To make the corner setting triangles, sew a red square to the end of a polka-dot rectangle. Add a gray tone-on-tone rectangle to the opposite side of the red square. Press both seam allowances toward the polka-dot fabric. Make four.

Make 4.

7. Align the right-angle corner of a gray tone-on-tone triangle with the polka-dot end of the sashing piece. Starting at the corner, sew the seam and press the seam allowances toward the triangle. Add a second triangle to the opposite side. Press the seam allowances toward the triangle. Align a square ruler with the triangle edges and trim the rectangle to a point as shown. Make four corner triangles.

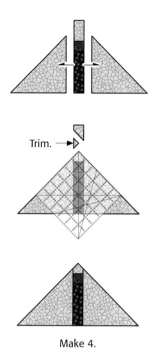

Make 4.

Assembling the Quilt Top

1. Working on a design wall and referring to the quilt diagram on the facing page, arrange the Four Patch blocks and the alternate blocks in a diagonal set. Move the blocks around until you're happy with the arrangement. Add the pieced side and corner setting triangles to the design wall.

2. Join the blocks and side triangles into rows. Press the seam allowances toward the alternate blocks and setting triangles.

3. Join the diagonal rows. Press the seam allowances open. Add the corner triangles and press the seam allowances toward the corner triangles.

4. Note that the red squares in the setting triangles are closer to the quilt edge than the Four Patch blocks. The quilt needs to be trimmed ¼" from the red squares. Trim and square up the quilt top, making sure to leave ¼" beyond the points of the red squares for seam allowance.

5. Cut two gray tone-on-tone 1½" x 42" strips into two equal lengths to make four shorter strips. Using a diagonal seam, join each of the shorter strips to the remaining four 42"-long border strips. Referring to "Borders with Butted Corners" on page 91, measure and cut the strips, and sew them to the sides and then to the top and bottom of the quilt top for the inner border.

6. Repeat step 5 using the six red 1½"-wide strips.

7. Measure and cut the black-and-gray floral 7"-wide strips, and sew them to the quilt top for the outer border. Press all seam allowances toward the outer border.

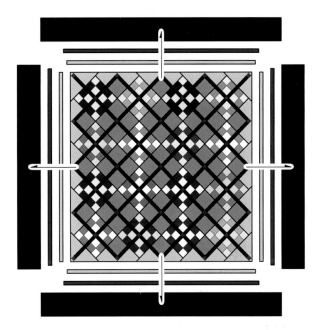

Finishing the Quilt

Refer to "Finishing" on page 93 for detailed instructions, if needed.

1. Piece the quilt backing so that it is 4" to 6" longer and wider than the quilt top.

2. Layer the quilt top with backing and batting. Baste with thread for hand quilting or with safety pins for machine quilting. If you're taking your quilt to a long-arm quilter, you do not need to layer and baste it.

3. Hand or machine quilt as desired.

4. Trim the batting and backing so that the edges are even with the quilt top. Use the medium gray 2½"-wide strips to bind the edges of the quilt.

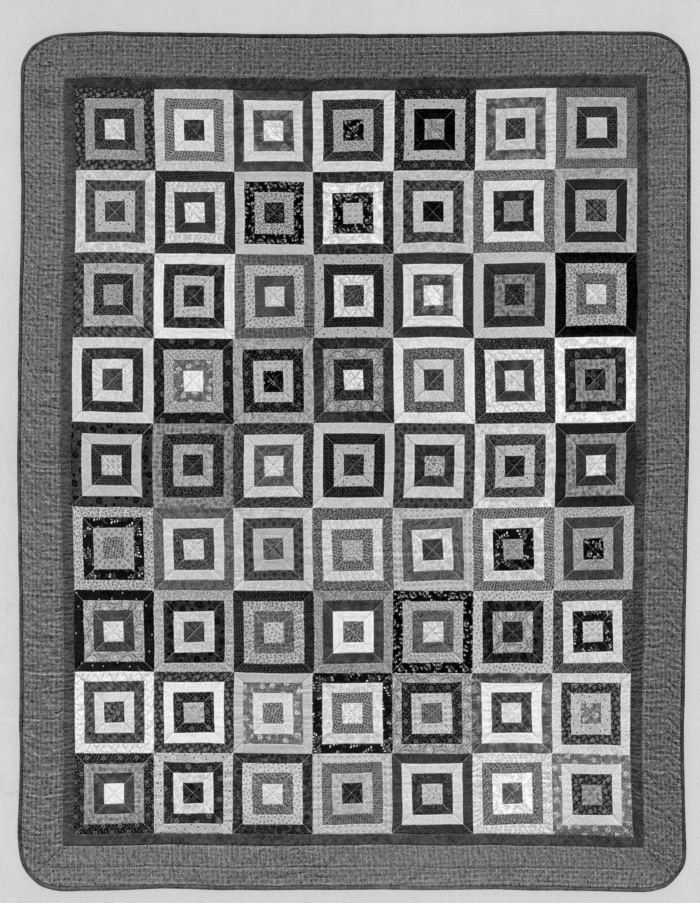

Made by Evelyn Sloppy

Apple Crisp

All the delicious browns in this quilt bring to mind thoughts of cinnamon, gingerbread, and apple crisp. The size makes it a great lap quilt to cuddle up with on cold winter evenings. In this quilt there are 63 Courthouse Steps blocks, set seven across and nine down.

Finished quilt size: 66" x 82"
Finished block size: 8" x 8"

Materials

Yardage is based on 42"-wide fabric.

½ yard *each* of 8 assorted medium-to-dark brown prints or 4 yards *total* of scraps for blocks

½ yard *each* of 8 assorted light brown prints or 4 yards *total* of scraps for blocks

⅜ yard of dark brown print for inner border

1 yard of medium brown print for outer border

¾ yard of fabric for binding

5 yards of fabric for backing

72" x 88" piece of batting

Cutting

From *each* of the 8 assorted medium-to-dark brown prints, cut:
- 1 strip, 2½" x 42"; crosscut into 4 squares, 2½" x 2½" (32 total, 1 is extra)
- 8 strips, 1½" x 42" (64 total)

From *each* of the 8 assorted light brown prints, cut:
- 1 strip, 2½" x 42"; crosscut into 4 squares, 2½" x 2½" (32 total)
- 8 strips, 1½" x 42" (64 total)

From the dark brown print, cut:
- 7 strips, 1½" x 42"

From the medium brown print, cut:
- 7 strips, 4½" x 42"

From the binding fabric, cut:
- 8 strips, 2½" x 42" (or 310" of 2½"-wide bias strips)

THE SCRAPPIER THE BETTER!

This quilt cries out for lots of scraps. Use as many as you can.

Making the Blocks

Each Courthouse Steps block consists of a 2½" square surrounded by three rings. Each ring consists of four pieces cut from the same fabric.

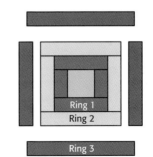
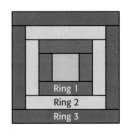

1. From each group of eight 1½"-wide strips cut from the 8 medium-to-dark brown prints and 8 light brown prints, cut enough pieces to make four sets of ring 1, four sets of ring 2, and four sets of ring 3, as shown:

Number to cut	Length
8	2½"
16	4½"
16	6½"
8	8½"

Keep each ring set together. Ring 1 requires 2½"- and 4½"-long strips. Ring 2 uses 4½"- and 6½"-long strips. And ring 3 calls for 6½"- and 8½"-long strips. You have cut enough pieces to make 64 blocks, but only 63 blocks will be needed. Discard the extras or save them for another project.

2. Starting with a 2½" light brown square, sew matching 1½" x 2½" medium-to-dark brown strips to opposite sides of the square. Then add matching 1½" x 4½" medium-to-dark brown strips to the other two sides of the square. Press the seam allowances toward the newly added strips. Making sure that each ring consists of only one fabric, continue for rings 2 and 3, alternating the medium-to-dark brown and light brown prints. Each block should measure 8½" x 8½". Make 32 blocks.

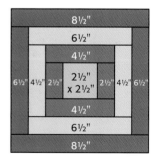

Make 32.

3. In the same manner, make 31 blocks starting with a 2½" medium-to-dark square and alternating the light brown and medium-to-dark brown prints for rings 1, 2, and 3.

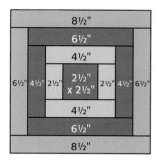

Make 31.

Assembling the Quilt

1. Join the Courthouse Steps blocks into nine rows of seven blocks each, alternating the light and dark blocks as shown. Press the seam allowances in opposite directions from row to row. Sew the rows together and press the seam allowances in one direction.

2. Sew the 1½"-wide dark brown strips together end to end. Sew the 4½"-wide medium brown strips together end to end. Referring to "Borders with Mitered Corners" on page 92, measure and cut the strips, and sew them to the quilt top for the inner and outer borders.

Finishing the Quilt

Refer to "Finishing" on page 93 for detailed instructions, if needed.

1. Piece the quilt backing so that it is 4" to 6" longer and wider than the quilt top.

2. Layer the quilt top with backing and batting. Baste with thread for hand quilting or with safety pins for machine quilting. If you're taking your quilt to a long-arm quilter, you do not need to layer and baste it.

3. Hand or machine quilt as desired.

4. Trim the batting and backing so that the edges are even with the quilt top. To make the quilt with rounded corners as shown on page 58, trim the corners with a dinner plate as a guide. Use the 2½"-wide binding strips to bind the edges of the quilt. At each curve, pin carefully so as not to stretch the binding. Note that you must use bias binding rather than straight-grain binding if you choose to make rounded corners.

SNUGGLE UP

Consider using flannel for the backing on lap quilts, even if you don't use it for the top. It makes a lap quilt feel so warm and cozy.

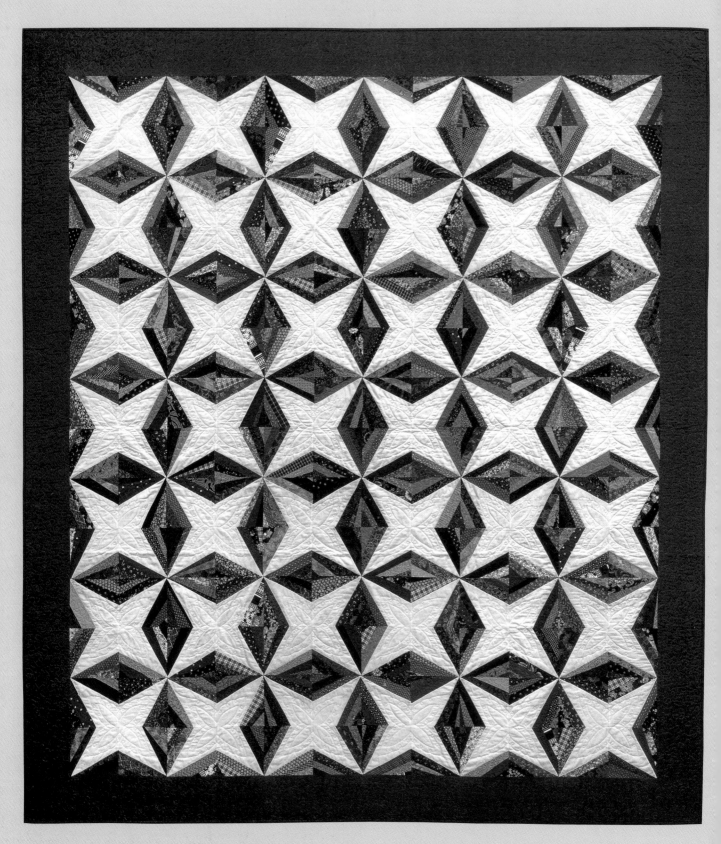

Pieced by Gayle Bong and the Crazy Quilters Quilt Guild; quilted by Cheryl Gerbing

Fractured Diamonds

This popular design uses scraps of varying widths sewn to a fabric foundation that stays in place and shows through as the light four-pointed star. Medium and dark scraps in any and all colors can be used, or you can limit yourself to just one color. The blocks in the quilt shown are 13" finished, but the pattern has been adjusted for 12" finished blocks to make better use of the fabric.

Finished quilt size: 84½" x 96½"
Finished block size: 12" x 12"

Materials

Yardage is based on 42"-wide fabric.
6 yards *total* of assorted medium and dark scraps for pieced diamonds
5½ yards of white fabric for foundation and star points
3 yards of blue print for border
¾ yard of fabric for binding
7¾ yards of fabric for backing
91" x 103" piece of batting

Cutting

From the white fabric, cut:
- 28 strips, 6½" x 42"; crosscut into 168 squares, 6½" x 6½"

From the medium and dark scraps, cut:
- 1,008 pieces, 1" to 2" wide x 3" (or longer)

From the *lengthwise grain* of the blue print, cut:
- 4 strips, 6½" x 100"

From the binding fabric, cut:
- 10 strips, 2¼" x 42"

Making the Blocks

1. Use a pencil and ruler to mark placement lines for the strips on the right side of each white square. To do this, mark a dot where the ¼" seam lines meet in one corner. Align the ¼" line of the ruler on the dot you've just marked and the 3" line of the ruler on the opposite corner and draw a line. Repeat on the adjacent side of the square as shown. Mark all 168 squares this way.

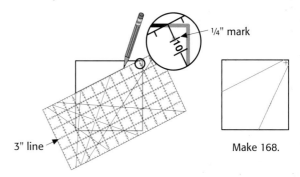

3" line   ¼" mark   Make 168.

TEMPLATE SAVES TIME

You could make a template to mark the placement lines on the blocks. Cut a 6½" square of template material and draw the lines as directed in step 1. Cut away the triangles on opposite sides of the square and use the remaining kite-shaped piece to mark your lines.

2. With right sides together, place the raw edge of a medium or dark scrap on the marked line as shown. (The bulk of the strip should fall toward the middle of the square.) Make sure both ends of the scrap extend past the foundation. Stitch ¼" from the raw edge of the strip. Flip the strip to the right side, covering the line you marked, and press. Trim both ends of the strip even with the foundation.

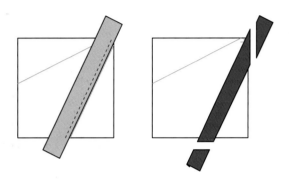

A SNIP IN TIME

To save time, make a rough cut with scissors, and then trim all the strips perfectly even with the foundation after the square is completed in step 4.

3. Place the next strip at a *slight* angle to the first strip, again making sure the ends of the scrap extend past the foundation. Sew, flip, press, and trim. Repeat with at least one more strip, or until the side of the foundation is covered.

4. Repeat steps 2 and 3 on the other line marked on the foundation. Arrange the strips to be nearly parallel, placing the end of the second and third strip a bit closer to the point where the strips meet. The seams of the first strips will overlap in the corner. This point where they meet will show you the exact ¼" seam allowance needed to create crisp star points when the blocks are sewn together. Repeat with all 168 foundations. Trim all the squares even with the foundation if you have not already done so.

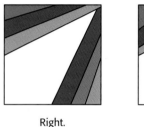

Right.   Wrong.

Slant strips with the narrow ends near the white point, not with the wide ends near the white point.

5. Align the raw edges of four foundation squares as shown to make a star. Join the squares into pairs, and then join the pairs to complete the block. Make 42 blocks.

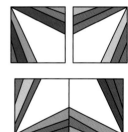
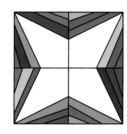

Make 42.

Assembling the Quilt Top

1. Arrange the blocks in seven rows of six blocks each as shown in the quilt assembly diagram. When you're happy with the color arrangement, sew the blocks into rows. Press the seam allowances in opposite directions from row to row. Sew the rows together and press the seam allowances in one direction.

2. Use the 6½"-wide blue strips to sew the border to the quilt top. The quilt shown has mitered borders; refer to "Adding Borders" on page 91 to attach your borders using whatever method you prefer.

Quilt assembly

Finishing the Quilt

Refer to "Finishing" on page 93 for detailed instructions, if needed.

1. Piece the quilt backing so that it is 4" to 6" longer and wider than the quilt top.

2. Layer the quilt top with backing and batting. Baste with thread for hand quilting or with safety pins for machine quilting. If you're taking your quilt to a long-arm quilter, you do not need to layer and baste it.

3. Hand or machine quilt as desired. Follow the quilting suggestion shown or use your own design.

4. Trim the batting and backing so that the edges are even with the quilt top. Use the 2¼"-wide binding strips to bind the edges of the quilt.

Made by Cyndi Walker

Cherry Cobbler

Fresh cherries are a favorite of Cyndi's and are twice as nice when worked into a quilt! Gingham ribbon, appliqué cherries, and a crisp color palette of red and white conjure images of picnics and lazy days in the park enjoying family and friends.

Finished quilt size: 62½" x 82½"
Finished block size: 10" x 10"

Materials

Yardage is based on 42"-wide fabric.

3⅝ yards *total* of assorted white and cream prints for blocks

2⅛ yards *total* of assorted red prints for Pinwheel blocks, cherry appliqués, and inner border

1 yard of red print for outer border

⅓ yard *total* of assorted green prints for leaf appliqués

⅔ yard of fabric for binding

5¼ yards of fabric for backing

69" x 89" piece of batting

6 yards of ¼"-wide red-and-white gingham ribbon for cherry stems

1¼ yards of 18"-wide fusible web

Water-soluble glue

Thread in coordinating colors for appliqué

Polyester monofilament

Cutting

From the assorted red prints, cut *a total of*:
- 10 strips, 2½" x 42"
- 6 strips, 1½" x 42"
- 36 squares, 3⅞" x 3⅞"; cut each square in half diagonally to make 72 triangles
- 4 squares, 2½" x 2½"

From the assorted white and cream prints, cut *a total*:
- 6 strips, 1½" x 42"
- 36 squares, 3⅞" x 3⅞"; cut each square in half diagonally to make 72 triangles
- 72 rectangles, 2½" x 6½"
- 17 squares, 11½" x 11½"

From the red print for the outer border, cut:
- 7 strips, 4½" x 42"

From the binding fabric, cut:
- 8 strips, 2½" x 42"

From the gingham ribbon, cut:
- 51 pieces, ¼" x 4"

Making the Pinwheel Blocks

1. With right sides together, sew one red half-square triangle and one white or cream half-square triangle together along their diagonal edges as shown; press. Make 72 scrappy half-square-triangle units.

Make 72.

2. Arrange four half-square-triangle units from step 1 as shown. Sew the units in each row together; press. Sew the rows together; press. Make 18 scrappy pinwheel units.

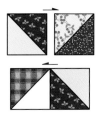

Make 18.

3. Sew one 1½"-wide red strip and one 1½"-wide white or cream strip together along their long edges to make a strip set as shown; press. Make six scrappy strip sets. Crosscut the strip sets into a total of 144 segments, 1½" wide. Arrange and sew two segments together as shown to make a four-patch unit; press. Make 72 scrappy four-patch units.

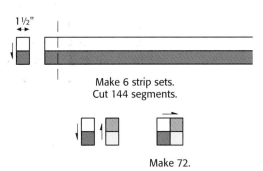

Make 6 strip sets.
Cut 144 segments.

Make 72.

4. Referring to the block assembly diagram below, arrange one unit from step 2, four units from step 3, and four 2½" x 6½" white or cream rectangles as shown. Sew the units and rectangles together into rows; press. Sew the rows together to complete the block; press. Make 18 blocks. Each block should measure 10½" x 10½".

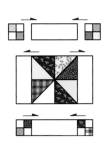

Make 18.

Making the Cherry Blocks

1. Referring to "Fusible Appliqué" on pages 89, use the patterns on page 70 to prepare 51 cherry appliqués (A) using the assorted red prints and 17 regular and 17 reversed leaf appliqués (B) using the assorted green prints.

2. Referring to the appliqué placement diagram below, use a small amount of water-soluble glue to tack three ¼" x 4" gingham stem pieces in place on each 11½" white or cream square, trimming the stems as necessary. Position and fuse three cherry appliqués (A) and one regular and one reversed leaf appliqué (B) on each block, tucking the ends of the stems under the edges of the cherries and leaves; allow the appliqués to cool. Use coordinating thread to machine blanket stitch around the edges of each cherry and leaf. Use polyester monofilament to zigzag stitch the stems in place. Make 17 blocks.

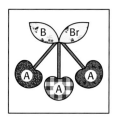

Appliqué placement diagram

3. Trim each Cherry block to 10½" x 10½", referring to "Squaring Up Blocks" on page 91 as needed.

Assembling the Quilt Top

1. Referring to the quilt assembly diagram, arrange the Pinwheel and Cherry blocks in seven rows of five blocks each, alternating them as shown. Sew the blocks together into rows. Press the seam allowances in opposite

directions from row to row. Sew the rows together to complete the quilt center; press.

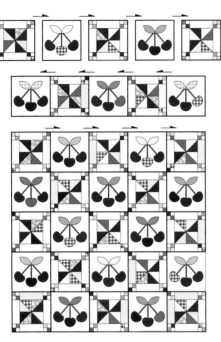

Assembly diagram

2. Arrange and sew five 2½"-wide assorted red strips together along their long edges to make a strip set as shown; press. Make two strip sets. Crosscut the strip sets into a total of 24 segments, 2½" wide.

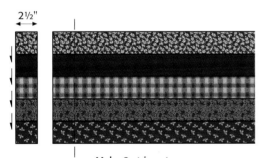

2½"

Make 2 strip sets.
Cut 24 segments.

3. Sew seven segments from step 2 together end to end to make one side inner-border strip as shown; press. Make two and sew them to the sides of the quilt. Press the seam allowances toward the border.

Make 2.

4. Sew two 2½" red squares and five segments from step 2 together to make a top inner-border strip as shown; press. Repeat to make a bottom inner-border strip.

Make 2.

5. Sew the top and bottom inner-border strips from step 4 to the top and bottom of the quilt; press.

6. Sew the 4½"-wide red strips together end to end. Referring to "Borders with Butted Corners" on page 91, measure and cut the strips, and sew them to the sides and then to the top and bottom of the quilt top for the outer border.

Finishing the Quilt

Refer to "Finishing" on page 93 for detailed instructions, if needed.

1. Piece the quilt backing so that it is 4" to 6" longer and wider than the quilt top.

2. Layer the quilt top with backing and batting. Baste with thread for hand quilting or with safety pins for machine quilting. If you're taking your quilt to a long-arm quilter, you do not need to layer and baste it.

3. Hand or machine quilt as desired.

4. Trim the batting and backing so that the edges are even with the quilt top. Use the 2½"-wide binding strips to bind the edges of the quilt.

Patterns do not include seam allowances.

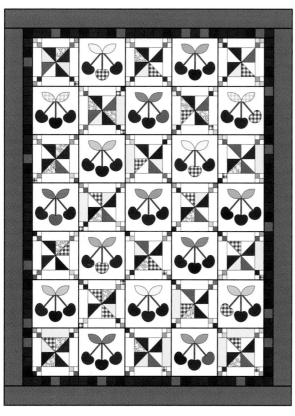

Quilt plan

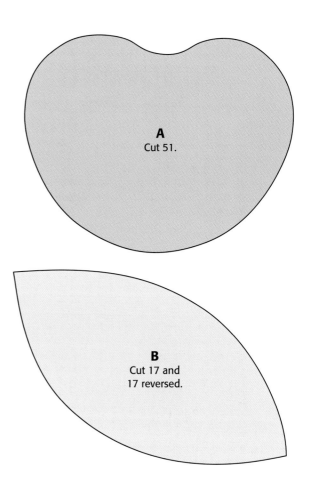

A
Cut 51.

B
Cut 17 and
17 reversed.

Stars over Mitford

Just like the stars in the sky, the stars in this quilt are there—you just don't always see them. Made with 1800s reproduction fabrics, this quilt is a great exercise tool for working with the placement of dark- and medium-value fabrics in a block. The instructions include several examples for the alternate placement of dark- and medium-value fabrics; use these, or create your own and have fun playing with your fabrics!

Finished quilt size: 71" x 95"
Finished block size: 12" x 12"

Materials

Yardage is based on 42"-wide fabric.
105 different pairs of squares, 5" x 5", of assorted dark and/or medium fabrics for blocks

35 squares, 5" x 5", of assorted dark and/or medium fabrics for blocks

70 different pairs of squares, 5" x 5", of assorted light fabrics for blocks

35 squares, 5" x 5", of assorted light fabrics for blocks

½ yard of medium fabric for inner border

2⅛ yards of dark fabric for outer border and binding

5⅞ yards of fabric for backing

77" x 101" piece of batting

Cutting

From the medium fabric for inner border, cut:
* 8 strips, 1½" x 42"

From the dark fabric for outer border and binding, cut:
* 9 strips, 4¾" x 42"
* 9 strips, 2½" x 42"

Making the Blocks

For each block, you'll use:
* 3 different pairs of assorted dark or medium 5" squares
* 1 assorted dark or medium 5" square
* 2 different pairs of assorted light 5" squares
* 1 assorted light 5" square

1. Refer to "Half-Square-Triangle Units" on page 85. Using one pair of dark or medium 5" squares and one pair of light squares, draw a diagonal line on the wrong side of each light square, and layer the squares with the dark squares to make

Made by Pat Speth

four half-square-triangle units. Press the seam allowances toward the light fabric. Trim the units to 4½" x 4½".

Make 4.

2. Cut one pair of dark or medium 5" squares into 2½" squares and one pair of light 5" squares into 2½" x 4½" rectangles. Refer to "Flying-Geese Units" on page 86. Draw a diagonal line on the wrong side of each 2½" background square. Use the marked squares and the rectangles to make four flying-geese units.

Make 4.

3. Trim ½" from one edge of one pair of dark or medium 5" squares. Cut the trimmed pieces in half in the opposite direction of the first cut to yield four rectangles, 2½" x 4½".

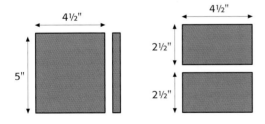

4. Sew a rectangle from step 3 to each flying-geese unit from step 2 as shown. Press the seam allowances toward the rectangles.

5. Trim a dark or medium 5" square to 4½" x 4½". Cut a light 5" square in half lengthwise and crosswise to yield four 2½" squares. Draw a diagonal line on the wrong side of the 2½" squares.

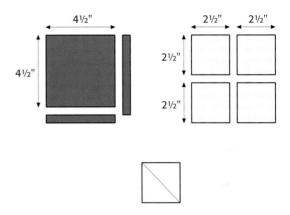

6. Position marked light squares on diagonally opposite corners of the medium 4½" square, right sides together. Sew along the line and trim away the corner fabric, leaving a ¼" seam allowance, and press as shown. Repeat, sewing light squares to the remaining two corners of the medium square; trim and press.

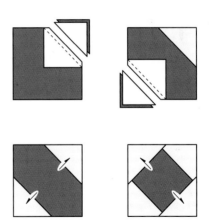

7. Arrange the four half-square-triangle units from step 1, the four flying-geese units from step 4, and the unit from step 6 into three horizontal rows as shown. Sew the units in each row together; press the seam allowances as indicated. Sew the rows together; press the seam allowances as indicated.

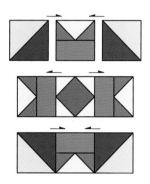

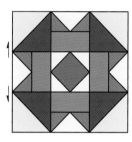

Stars over Mitford block

8. Repeat steps 1–7 to make a total of 35 blocks, using the diagrams below for alternate placement of the dark and medium fabrics if desired.

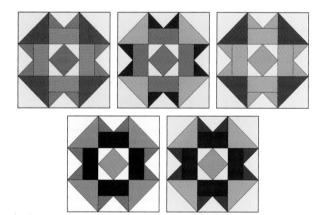

Assembling the Quilt Top

1. Refer to the quilt plan to arrange the blocks in seven rows of five blocks each on your design wall. Sew the blocks in each row together; press the seam allowances in opposite directions from row to row. Sew the rows together; press the seam allowances in one direction.

2. Sew the medium 1½"-wide strips together end to end. Referring to "Borders with Butted Corners" on page 91, measure and cut the strips, and

sew them to the sides and then to the top and bottom of the quilt top for the inner border.

3. Sew the dark 4¾"-wide strips together end to end. Measure and cut the strips, and sew them to the quilt top for the outer border.

Quilt plan

Finishing the Quilt

Refer to "Finishing" on page 93 for detailed instructions, if needed.

1. Piece the quilt backing so that it is 4" to 6" longer and wider than the quilt top.

2. Layer the quilt top with backing and batting. Baste with thread for hand quilting or with safety pins for machine quilting. If you're taking your quilt to a long-arm quilter, you do not need to layer and baste it.

3. Hand or machine quilt as desired.

4. Trim the batting and backing so that the edges are even with the quilt top. Use the dark 2½"-wide strips to bind the edges of the quilt.

Idaho Farm Girl

eAwash with color and soft as a gentle rain, this quilt blooms with all the modest charm of a farmhouse garden. Wrap yourself in warmth and sit a spell as the virtues of country living soothe your soul.

Finished quilt size: 65½" x 65½"
Finished block size: 5" x 5"

Materials

Yardage is based on 42"-wide fabric.

3½ yards *total* of assorted cream prints for block backgrounds

3⅛ yards *total* of assorted light, medium, and dark prints for blocks

2 yards *total* of assorted red prints for blocks and binding

4 yards of fabric for backing

72" x 72" piece of batting

Cutting

To simplify the process, cutting instructions are provided separately for each type of block. Depending upon the number of prints you have on hand, you may wish to cut more than one set from some of the assorted light, medium, and dark prints, and from the assorted red prints as well, to produce the required number of pieces. The assorted cream background prints are used randomly within each block for a scrappy "make do" look.

SNOWBALL VARIATION BLOCK

From the assorted cream prints, cut a total of:
- 864 squares, 1½" x 1½"

From the assorted light, medium, and dark prints, cut *a total of*:
- 432 squares, 3" x 3", in matching sets of 4

FARMER'S DAUGHTER BLOCK

From the assorted red prints, cut *a total of*:
- 793 squares, 1½" x 1½", in matching sets of 13

From the assorted cream prints, cut *a total of*:
- 488 squares, 1½" x 1½"
- 244 rectangles, 1½" x 3½"

BINDING

From the assorted red prints, cut:
- Enough 2½"-wide random lengths to make 272" of binding

Making the Snowball Variation Blocks

1. Using a mechanical pencil, draw a diagonal line on the wrong side of the 864 assorted cream print 1½" background squares.

Designed by Kim Diehl; machine pieced by Evelyne Schow; machine quilted by Kathy Ockerman

SIMPLE DIAGONAL STITCHING

To eliminate drawing lines on the wrong side of small squares, you can use tape to mark the center sewing line of your machine as follows:

1. Lower the needle to the "down" position and gently place an acrylic ruler on the sewing surface, with the left edge resting against the needle. Ensure the ruler is aligned in a straight position and lower the presser foot to hold it in place.

2. Place a length of 4" masking tape exactly along the ruler's edge, extending it to the front edge of the sewing machine surface; take care not to cover the feed dogs.

3. Place the top point of the layered fabric square at the needle, and align the bottom point with the right edge of the tape as you stitch from end to end. The resulting diagonal seam will be positioned precisely down the center of the square.

2. Select one set of four matching 3" squares. With right sides together, layer a prepared 1½" background square over one corner of each 3" square in the set. Referring to "Chain Piecing" on page 85, stitch each layered pair together exactly on the drawn line.

Make 4.

3. Repeat step 2, placing a prepared 1½" background square on the opposite corner of each 3" square.

Make 4.

4. Fold the top triangle back and align its corner with the corner of the bottom piece of fabric to keep it square; press in place. Trim away the excess layers of fabric beneath the top triangle, leaving a ¼" seam allowance. Repeat for a total of four units.

Make 4.

5. Lay out the pieced units in two horizontal rows to form a Snowball Variation block. Join the pieces in each row. Press the seam allowances in opposite directions. Join the block halves. Press the seam allowances open.

6. Repeat steps 2–5 using the remaining sets of 3" light, medium, and dark print squares. Make a total of 108 Snowball Variation blocks measuring 5½" x 5½".

Making the Farmer's Daughter Blocks

1. Select one set of 13 matching red print 1½" squares. Lay out five red print squares and four 1½" cream print squares in three horizontal rows to form a nine-patch unit. Join the pieces in each row. Press the seam allowances toward the red print. Join the rows. Press the seam allowances away from the center row.

2. Draw a diagonal line on the wrong side of the eight remaining red print 1½" squares.

3. With right sides together, align a prepared red print square on each opposite end of a cream print 1½" x 3½" rectangle, placing them in mirror-image positions. Sew the layers together exactly on the drawn lines. Press and trim as instructed in step 4 of "Making the Snowball Variation Blocks" on page 77. Repeat for a total of four units.

Make 4.

4. Join units from step 3 to two opposite sides of the nine-patch unit. Press the seam allowances toward the nine-patch unit.

5. Sew a cream print 1½" square to each short end of the two remaining units from step 3. Press the seam allowances toward the cream print square.

6. Sew the units made in step 5 to the remaining sides of the nine-patch unit from step 4. Press the seam allowances toward the block center.

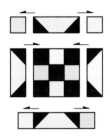 

7. Repeat steps 1–6 to make 61 Farmer's Daughter blocks measuring 5½" x 5½".

Making the Rows

1. Lay out 13 Snowball Variation blocks to make a row A. Join the blocks. Press the seam allowances all in one direction. Repeat to make a total of two A rows.

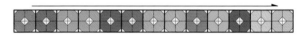

Row A.
Make 2.

2. Lay out seven Snowball Variation blocks and six Farmer's Daughter blocks in alternating positions to make a B row. Join the blocks. Press the seam allowances toward the Snowball Variation blocks. Repeat to make a total of six B rows.

Row B.
Make 6.

3. Lay out eight Snowball Variation blocks and five Farmer's Daughter blocks as shown to make a C row. Join the blocks. Press the seam allowances of the first and last Snowball Variation block toward the center of the row. Press the remaining seam allowances toward the Snowball Variation blocks. Repeat to make five C rows.

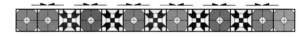

Row C.
Make 5.

Assembling the Quilt Top

1. Lay out six of row B and five of row C, alternating positions. Sew the rows together. Press the seam allowances open.

2. Join a row A to the top and bottom of the quilt top. Press the seam allowances toward the A rows. The pieced quilt top should now measure 65½" x 65½".

Finishing the Quilt

Refer to "Finishing" on page 93 for detailed instructions, if needed.

1. Piece the quilt backing so that it is 4" to 6" longer and wider than the quilt top.

2. Layer the quilt top with backing and batting. Baste with thread for hand quilting or with safety pins for machine quilting. If you're taking your quilt to a long-arm quilter, you do not need to layer and baste it.

3. Hand or machine quilt as desired.

4. Trim the batting and backing so that the edges are even with the quilt top. Join the 2½"-wide, random-length strips into one length and use it to bind the edges of the quilt.

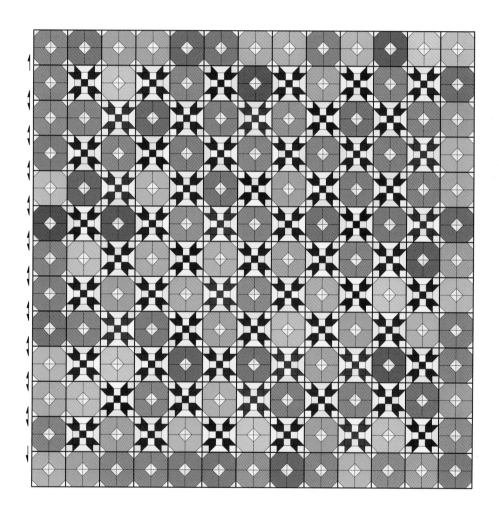

Made by Sally Schneider; quilted by Leona VanLeeuwen

Good Fences Make Good Neighbors

When Sally first saw this design in a photograph, it was done in Amish colors and looked quite complex and difficult to make. Further analysis, however, showed it to be a simple block in a diagonal setting. The name of the quilt comes from Robert Frost's poem *Mending Wall*, and refers to the scrap pinwheels kept separate by the Rail Fence strip between each group of colorful pinwheels.

Finished quilt size: 81¼" x 95½"
Finished block size: 10" x 10"

Materials

Yardage is based on 42"-wide fabric.

1⅞ yards *total* of assorted light prints for blocks

1⅞ yards *total* of assorted dark prints for blocks

2⅞ yards of navy print for Rail Fence strips and border

1⅓ yards of red print for Rail Fence strips

1½ yards of light print for setting triangles

¾ yard of red print for binding

7½ yards of backing

87" x 102" piece of batting

Cutting

From the assorted dark prints, cut *a total of*:
- 20 strips, 3" x 42"; crosscut into 200 rectangles, 3" x 4"

From the assorted light prints, cut *a total of*:
- 20 strips, 3" x 42"; crosscut into 200 rectangles, 3" x 4"

From the red print, cut:
- 4 strips, 10½" x 42"; crosscut into 50 rectangles, 3" x 10½"

From the navy print, cut:
- 4 strips, 10½" x 42"; crosscut into 50 rectangles, 3" x 10½"
- 9 strips, 5½" x 42"

From the light print for setting triangles, cut:
- 3 strips, 16" x 42"; crosscut into:
    - 5 squares, 16" x 16"; cut each square twice diagonally to yield 20 setting triangles (2 are extra)
    - 2 squares, 10" x 10"; cut each square in half diagonally to yield 4 corner triangles

From the red print for binding, cut:
- 9 strips, 2¼" x 42"

Making the Blocks

After sewing each seam, press the seam allowances in the direction indicated by the arrows.

1. Layer a light rectangle and a dark rectangle, right sides together, and draw 45° lines from opposite corners on the wrong side of the light rectangle as shown. Sew on both drawn lines, and then cut the rectangles apart between the lines. Press the seam allowances toward the darker fabric. Repeat to make four matching half-square-triangle units. Make a total of 400 half-square-triangle units.

Make 4 matching
half-square-triangle units.

2. Lay out a set of four matching half-square-triangle units in a four-patch arrangement. Make sure you keep the light and dark triangles always rotating in the same direction; otherwise some of your pinwheels will spin in the opposite direction. Sew the units together in pairs, and then sew the pairs together to complete the pinwheel units. Make a total of 100 pinwheel units.

Make 100.

3. Sew pinwheel units together in pairs to make 50 block centers.

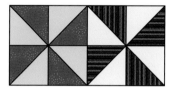

Make 50.

4. Sew a navy rectangle to one long side of each block center, and then sew a red rectangle to the opposite side. Make 50 blocks measuring 10½" x 10½".

Make 50.

Assembling the Quilt Top

1. Lay out the blocks and the light side and corner setting triangles as shown in the quilt layout diagram on the facing page. Make sure to arrange the blocks to keep the lines of color zigzagging across the quilt top.

2. When you're satisfied with the block arrangement, sew the blocks and side triangles together into diagonal rows. Press the seam allowances in opposite directions from row to row. Sew the rows together. Add the corner triangles last and press. The setting triangles were cut a bit oversized for easier cutting and

piecing. Trim and square up the quilt top, making sure to leave ¼" beyond the points of all blocks for seam allowances.

3. Sew the 5½"-wide navy strips together end to end. Referring to "Borders with Butted Corners" on page 91, measure and cut the strips, and sew them to the sides and then to the top and bottom of the quilt top for the outer border. Press all seam allowances toward the border.

Finishing the Quilt

Refer to "Finishing" on page 93 for detailed instructions, if needed.

1. Piece the quilt backing so that it is 4" to 6" longer and wider than the quilt top.

2. Layer the quilt top with backing and batting. Baste with thread for hand quilting or with safety pins for machine quilting. If you're taking your quilt to a long-arm quilter, you do not need to layer and baste it.

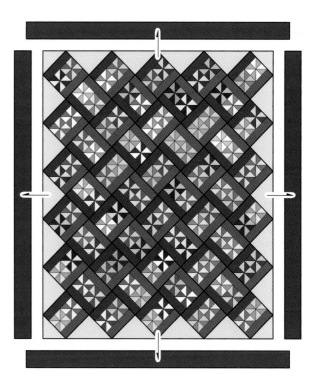

3. Hand or machine quilt as desired. See the quilting suggestion below.

Quilting diagram

4. Trim the batting and backing so that the edges are even with the quilt top. Use the 2¼"-wide red strips to bind the edges of the quilt.

Quiltmaking Basics

From choosing fabrics to binding, you'll find this section filled with helpful information that can make putting your quilt together a pleasurable experience.

Remove the square ruler and cut along the right edge of the long ruler, rolling the rotary cutter away from you. Discard this strip. (Reverse this procedure if you are left-handed.)

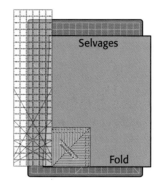

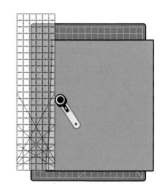

Fabrics

Select 100% cotton fabrics. They hold their shape well and are easy to handle. Cotton blends can be more difficult to stitch and press. Sometimes, however, a cotton blend is worth a little extra effort if it's the perfect fabric for your quilt.

Yardage requirements are provided for all the projects in this book and are based on 42"-wide fabrics that provide at least 40" of usable fabric after prewashing. If you have a collection of scraps, feel free to use them and purchase only those fabrics you need to complete the quilt you're making.

Rotary Cutting

Instructions for quick-and-easy rotary cutting are provided wherever possible. All measurements include standard ¼"-wide seam allowances. For those unfamiliar with rotary cutting, a brief introduction is provided below.

1. To prepare the fabric, iron it to remove wrinkles. Fold the fabric and match selvages, aligning the crosswise and lengthwise grains as much as possible. Place the folded fabric on the cutting mat, with the folded edge closest to you.

2. Align a square ruler along the folded edge of the fabric. Then place a long, straight ruler to the left of the square ruler, just covering the uneven raw edges of the left side of the fabric.

3. To cut strips, align the required measurement on the ruler with the newly cut edge of the fabric. For example, to cut a 3"-wide strip, place the 3" ruler mark on the edge of the fabric.

4. To cut squares or rectangles, cut strips in the required widths. Trim away the selvage ends. Align the required measurement on the ruler with the left edge of the strip and cut a square or rectangle.

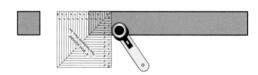

5. For half-square triangles, cut squares in half diagonally. For quarter-square triangles, cut squares twice diagonally.

Two half-square triangles cut from one square

Four quarter-square triangles cut from one square

CUTTING BIAS STRIPS

1. Position the fabric on the grid side of the cutting mat so that the lengthwise and crosswise grains of the fabric align with the vertical and horizontal grid lines.

2. Begin cutting approximately 6" from the lower-left corner of the fabric. Align the 45° line on the ruler with the first horizontal grid line visible on the mat below the fabric's bottom edge. Make a cut, creating a waste triangle.

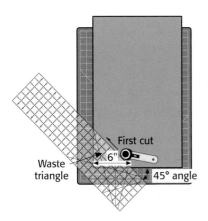

Waste triangle
First cut
6"
45° angle

3. Align the required measurement on your ruler with the newly cut edge and cut the first strip.

4. Continue cutting until you have the number of strips required. Periodically recheck the position of the 45° angle marking on the ruler. If necessary, retrim the cut edge of the fabric to "true up" the angle.

Machine Piecing

The most important thing to remember about machine piecing is to maintain a consistent ¼"-wide seam allowance. This is necessary for seams to match and for the resulting block or quilt to measure the desired finished size. Measurements for all components of each quilt are based on blocks that finish accurately to the desired size plus ¼" on each edge for seam allowances.

Take the time to establish an exact ¼"-wide seam guide on your machine. Some machines have a special quilting foot that measures exactly ¼" from the center needle position to the edge of the foot. If your machine doesn't have such a foot,

create a seam guide by placing the edge of a piece of tape or moleskin ¼" from the needle.

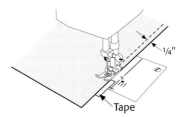

¼"

Tape

CHAIN PIECING

Chain piecing saves time and thread when you're sewing many identical units. Simply sew the first pair of pieces from cut edge to cut edge. At the end of the seam, stop sewing, but do not cut the thread. Feed the next pair of pieces under the presser foot, as close as possible to the first. Continue sewing without cutting threads. When all the pieces are sewn, remove the chain from the machine, clip the threads, and press.

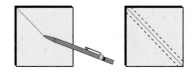

HALF-SQUARE-TRIANGLE UNITS

Here is a method of making half-square-triangle units that is fast and accurate.

1. Cut the squares the size specified in the cutting list.

2. Draw a diagonal line from corner to corner on the wrong side of the lighter fabric. Layer two same-sized squares right sides together with the marked square on top and raw edges aligned. Sew ¼" on each side of the drawn line.

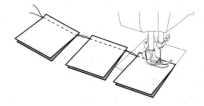

3. Cut on the drawn line. Press the seam allowances toward the darker fabric, unless instructed otherwise, and trim the dog-ears. Each pair of squares will yield two half-square-triangle units.

4. If your squares were cut oversized, use a square ruler to trim your half-square-triangle units to the correct unfinished size. Place the diagonal line of the ruler on the seam of the unit and trim two sides as shown. Rotate the block and trim the other two sides.

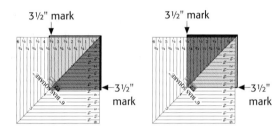

FLYING-GEESE UNITS

The only pieces you need to make these units are squares and rectangles.

1. Cut the squares and rectangles as directed in the project instructions. Draw a diagonal line from corner to corner on the wrong side of the squares as directed.

2. With right sides together, place a marked square on top of a rectangle at the right-hand end. Stitch one thread width to the outside of the diagonal line. Trim away the excess fabric, leaving a ¼" seam allowance. Press the seam allowances toward the resulting triangle.

3. Repeat step 2 to sew a second marked square to the left end of the rectangle and press.

Flying-geese unit

PAPER FOUNDATION PIECING

With foundation piecing, the pieces are sewn to a paper foundation that is marked with the block pattern or unit. Grain line is not as important to this method as in traditional piecing because the paper gives the block stability during sewing. Use a 90/14 sewing machine needle (this larger needle perforates the paper better), thread in a color that will blend, and a smaller-than-normal stitch length (about 15 stitches per inch).

1. Trace or copy the foundation pattern for the block or unit you'll be making. Trim the foundation, leaving at least ¼" of foundation around the outer (cutting) line—you'll trim the fabrics to leave an exact ¼" seam allowance after completely stitching each block or unit.

2. Following the project instructions, cut the fabric pieces for each block. The measurements listed for the individual pieces are slightly larger than needed. (It's better to have too much fabric to cut away than not enough to cover the area.)

3. Beginning with piece 1, place the first fabric piece right side up on the wrong of the pattern (the side without any lines). Hold the paper up to a light source to make sure the fabric piece is at least ¼" larger on all sides than area 1. Turn the paper and fabric over, being careful not to move the fabric, and pin the fabric in place through the marked side of the paper. Place the pin so that it does not extend into the seam line.

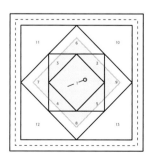

4. Once again, turn the foundation over to the wrong (or unmarked) side. Look through the paper and place the fabric for piece 2, right side up, over area 2. When the fabric for piece 2 is properly positioned, flip it on top of piece 1, right sides together. Make sure that piece 2 extends at least ¼" into area 2.

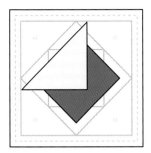

5. Hold the layers in place, turn the foundation over, and carefully position the unit under your sewing machine's presser foot. With the right (or marked) side of the paper foundation up and the fabrics on the bottom, sew on the line between areas 1 and 2, starting ¼" before the line and extending ¼" beyond. There is no need to backstitch.

6. Open piece 2 and remove the pin from piece 1. Hold the block up to the light source and look through the fabric to be sure the edges of piece 2 extend beyond the seam lines for area 2 on the foundation. Refold the fabrics with right sides together and then fold the paper back to reveal the seam allowance. Place a ruler along the edge of the paper and trim the seam allowances to ¼". Open the fabrics so that both pieces are right side up and press the seam allowances to one side with a dry iron.

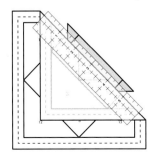 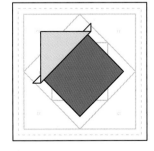

7. Fold the paper back along the next seam line. Trim the fabric so that it extends ¼" past this fold line. This trimming creates a straight edge upon which you can line up your next fabric piece, making placement much easier.

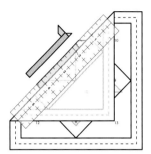

8. Continue in this manner, adding pieces in numerical order until the pattern is completely covered with fabric pieces.

9. Use a rotary cutter to trim away the excess fabric around the unit, leaving a ¼" seam allowance all around. Gently remove the paper foundation.

Appliqué

There are many techniques for appliqué and there's not space to cover all of them here. For information on other methods or more details, consult some of the many excellent books on the topic, or visit your local quilt shop to look into classes.

MAKING TEMPLATES

To make permanent plastic templates, place template plastic over each pattern piece and trace with a fine-line permanent marker. Seam allowances are not included on templates for appliqué pieces. Piecing template patterns include the seam allowance, which is shown as part of the template. Cut out the templates on the drawn lines. You need only one template for each different motif or shape. Mark the pattern name, grain line, and piece number (if applicable) on the templates.

FREEZER PAPER FOR HAND OR MACHINE APPLIQUÉ

This method of preparing appliqué shapes can be used for both hand appliqué and machine appliqué.

1. Trace the appliqué pattern onto the dull side of freezer paper. Trace the pattern in reverse if it's asymmetrical and has not already been reversed for tracing. For symmetrical patterns, it doesn't matter.

2. Cut out the freezer-paper template on the drawn lines and press it to the wrong side of the appliqué fabric.

3. Cut out the fabric shapes, adding a scant ¼" seam allowance around each shape.

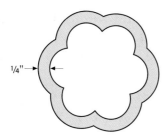

4. Turn the seam allowance over the edge of the paper and baste it to the paper. Clip the corners and baste inner curves first. On outer curves, take small running stitches through the fabric only, to ease in fullness. Do not turn under edges that will be covered by another piece.

Do not turn under or baste seam allowance that is overlapped by another piece.

5. For sharp points, first fold the corner to the inside; then fold the remaining seam allowances over the paper.

Fold corners to inside.   Fold remaining seam allowances over paper.

6. When all seam allowances are turned and basted, press the appliqués.

7. Pin and stitch the pieces to the background by hand or machine.

8. After stitching, remove the basting stitches, carefully slit the background fabric behind the appliqué shape, and pull out the paper. Use tweezers if necessary to loosen the freezer paper.

NEEDLE-TURN HAND APPLIQUÉ

Use a longer needle, a Sharp or milliner's needle, to help you control the seam allowance and turn it under as you stitch.

1. Place the template right side up on the right side of the fabric and trace around it with a No. 2 pencil or a white pencil, depending on your fabric color and print.

2. Cut the shape out, adding a scant ¼" seam allowance all around.

3. Pin or baste the appliqué piece in position on the background fabric.

4. Beginning on a straight edge, bring your needle up through the background and the appliqué piece, just inside the drawn line. Use the tip of the needle to gently turn under the seam allowance, about ½" at a time. Hold the turned seam allowance firmly between the thumb and first finger of one hand as you stitch the

appliqué to the background fabric with your other hand. Use the traditional appliqué stitch described next.

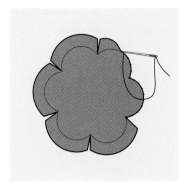

TRADITIONAL APPLIQUÉ STITCH

1. Thread a needle with a single strand of thread and knot one end. Use a thread color that matches the appliqué piece.

2. Slip the needle into the seam allowance from the wrong side of the appliqué, bringing it out on the fold line. Start the first stitch by inserting the needle into the background fabric right next to the folded edge of the appliqué where the thread exits the appliqué shape.

3. Let the needle travel under the background fabric, parallel to the edge of the appliqué; bring the needle up about ⅛" away through the edge of the appliqué, catching only one or two threads of the folded edge. Insert the needle into the background fabric right next to the folded edge. Let the needle travel under the background, and again, bring it up about ⅛" away, catching just the edge of the appliqué. Give the thread a slight tug and continue stitching.

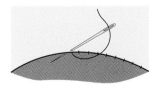

Appliqué stitch

4. Stitch around the appliqué, taking a couple of stitches beyond where you started. Knot the thread on the wrong side of the background fabric, behind the appliqué.

FUSIBLE APPLIQUÉ

This appliqué method is fast and easy. Many fusing products are available for applying one piece of fabric to another, but fabrics do stiffen after application, so choose a lightweight web. Follow the manufacturer's directions for the product you select. Unless the patterns are symmetrical or the pattern has already been reversed, you must *reverse the templates when you draw them onto the paper side of the fusible web.* Do not add seam allowances to the appliqué pieces.

1. Trace or draw your shape on the paper backing side of the fusible web. Cut out the shape, leaving a ¼" to ½" margin all around each shape.

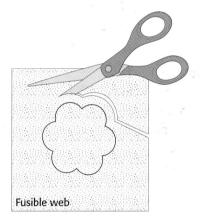

Fusible web

2. Fuse the shapes to the wrong side of your fabric. For large appliqués, you can cut out the center of the fusible web, leaving a "donut" of web so that the centers of your appliqués will remain soft and unfused.

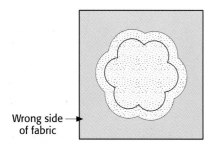

Wrong side of fabric

3. Cut out the shape exactly on the marked line.

4. Remove the paper backing, position the shape on the background, and press it in place with your iron.

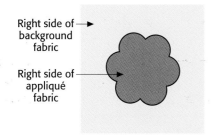

Right side of background fabric

Right side of appliqué fabric

5. For quilts that will be washed often, finish the edges of the appliqués by stitching around them with a decorative stitch, such as a blanket stitch (by hand or machine) or zigzag stitch.

MACHINE APPLIQUÉ

For the most "invisible" stitches, use monofilament–clear for light-colored appliqués or smoke for medium or dark colors. If you want your stitches to show as a more decorative element, use a matching or contrasting color thread in the top of your machine. Use a neutral-colored thread or thread to match your background fabric in the bobbin.

1. Set your machine for a small zigzag stitch (about $\frac{1}{16}$" wide) and do a practice sample to test your stitches and tension. An open-toe presser foot is helpful for machine appliqué.

2. Begin stitching with the needle just outside the appliqué piece and take two or three straight stitches in place first to lock the thread. Make sure the needle is on the right of the appliqué and that the zigzag stitches will go into the appliqué piece.

Note: You can use any decorative stitch on your machine.

3. Stitch curved shapes slowly to maintain control, stopping and pivoting as needed.

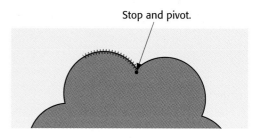

Stop and pivot.

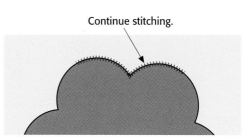

Continue stitching.

4. Stitch completely around the appliqué until you're slightly beyond the starting point. Take two or three straight stitches in place to lock the thread and clip the thread tails.

5. To remove freezer paper, carefully trim away the background fabric behind the appliqué, leaving a generous ¼" seam allowance to keep your appliqué secure. Use tweezers as needed. (Bias stems and vines and fused appliqué shapes will not have paper to remove, so it's not necessary to cut away the background.)

Squaring Up Blocks

When your blocks are complete, take time to square them up. Use a large square ruler to measure your blocks and make sure they're the desired size plus an exact ¼" seam allowance on each side. For example, if you are making 9" blocks, they should all measure 9½" before you sew them together. Trim the larger blocks to match the size of the smallest one. Be sure to trim all four sides, or your blocks will be lopsided.

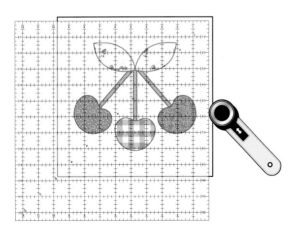

If your blocks aren't the required finished size, adjust all the other components of the quilt, such as sashing and borders, accordingly.

Adding Borders

For best results, do not cut border strips and sew them directly to the quilt without measuring first. Measure the quilt top through the center in both directions to determine how long to cut the border strips. This step ensures that the finished quilt will be as straight and as "square" as possible, without wavy edges.

Many of these quilts call for plain border strips. Some of these strips are cut along the crosswise grain and joined where extra length is needed. Others are cut lengthwise and do not need to be pieced.

BORDERS WITH BUTTED CORNERS

1. Measure the length of the quilt top through the center. Cut two borders to this measurement. Determine the midpoints of the border and quilt top by folding them in half and creasing or pinning the centers. Then pin the borders to opposite sides of the quilt top, matching the center marks and ends and easing as necessary. Sew the border strips in place. Press the seam allowances toward the borders.

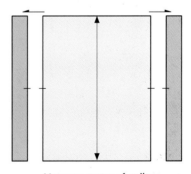

Measure center of quilt, top to bottom. Mark centers.

2. Measure the width of the quilt top through the center, including the side borders just added. Cut two borders to this measurement. Mark the centers of the quilt edges and the border strips. Pin the borders to the top and bottom edges of

the quilt top, matching the center marks and ends and easing as necessary. Sew the border strips in place. Press the seam allowances toward the borders.

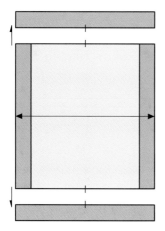

Measure center of quilt, side to side, including border strips. Mark centers.

BORDERS WITH MITERED CORNERS

1. Estimate the finished outside dimensions of your quilt, including the border. For example, if your quilt top measures 35½" x 50½" across the center and you want a 5"-wide border, your quilt will measure about 45" x 60" after the border is attached. Add at least ½" to these measurements for seam allowances. To give yourself some leeway, you may want to add an additional 3" to 4" to those measurements. In this example, you would then cut two border strips that measure approximately 48" long and two border strips that measure approximately 63" long.

   Note: *If your quilt has more than one border, you can sew all the border strips together for each side first, and then sew them all to the quilt top at once. When you're mitering the corners, be sure to match the seam intersections of each different border.*

2. Fold the quilt in half and mark the centers of the quilt edges. Fold each border strip in half and mark the centers with pins.

3. Measure the length and width of the quilt top across the center. Note the measurements.

4. Place a pin at each end of the side border strips to mark the length of the quilt top. Repeat with the top and bottom border strips.

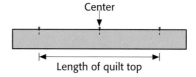

Center

Length of quilt top

5. Pin the border strips to the quilt top, matching the centers. Line up the pins at either end of the border strip with the edges of the quilt. Stitch, beginning and ending ¼" from the raw edges of the quilt top. Repeat with the remaining border strips.

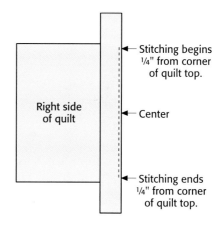

Right side of quilt

Stitching begins ¼" from corner of quilt top.

Center

Stitching ends ¼" from corner of quilt top.

6. Lay the first corner to be mitered on the ironing board. Fold under one border strip at a 45° angle to the other strip. Press and pin.

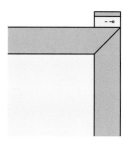

7. Fold the quilt with right sides together, lining up the adjacent edges of the border. If necessary, use a ruler and pencil to draw a line on the crease to make the stitching line more visible. Stitch on the pressed crease, sewing from the previous stitching line to the outside edges.

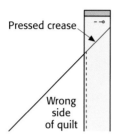

Pressed crease

Wrong side of quilt

8. Press the seam allowances open, check the right side of the quilt to make sure the miters are neat, and then turn the quilt over and trim away the excess border strips, leaving a ¼" seam allowance.

9. Repeat with the remaining corners.

Finishing

The quilt "sandwich" consists of backing, batting, and the quilt top. Cut the quilt backing 4" to 6" longer and wider than the quilt top. Baste together with thread for hand quilting or safety pins for machine quilting. Quilt by hand or machine.

BINDING

The quilt directions tell you how wide to cut the strips for binding. Bindings are generally cut anywhere from 2" to 2½" wide, depending on personal preference. You'll need enough strips to go around the perimeter of the quilt plus 12".

1. Sew the strips together end to end to make one long piece of binding. Join the strips at right angles and stitch from corner to corner. Trim the excess fabric and press the seam allowances open.

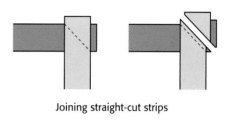

Joining straight-cut strips

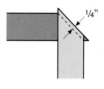

¼"

Joining bias strips

2. Trim one end of the binding strip at a 45° angle. Turn under ¼" and press.

3. Fold the strip in half lengthwise, wrong sides together, and press.

Fold line

4. Trim the batting and backing even with the quilt top.

5. Starting in the middle of one side and using a ¼"-wide seam allowance, stitch the binding to the quilt. Keep the raw edges even with the quilt-top edge. Begin stitching 1" to 2" from the start of the binding. End the stitching ¼" from the corner of the quilt and backstitch. Clip the thread.

6. Turn the quilt so that you'll be stitching along the next side. Fold the binding up, away from the quilt; then fold it back down onto itself, even with the raw edge of the quilt top.

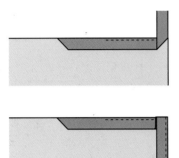

7. Stitch from the fold of the binding along the second edge of the quilt top, stopping ¼" from the corner as before. Repeat the stitching and mitering process on the remaining edges and corners.

8. When you reach the starting point, cut the end 1" longer than needed and tuck the end inside the beginning. Stitch the rest of the binding.

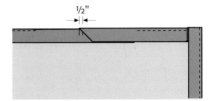

9. Fold the binding over the raw edges of the quilt to the back, with the folded edge covering the row of machine stitching. Hand stitch in place, mitering the corners.

About the Designers

GAYLE BONG

An avid quilter for more than 25 years, Gayle is the author of numerous quilting books. Her most recent release is *S is for Scraps*. Visit her at www.gaylebong.com and www.gaylebong.blogspot.com.

KIM BRACKETT

Kim began quilting in 1988 after admiring a collection of quilts in an antique shop. She has written two books, *Scrap-Basket Surprises* and *Scrap-Basket Sensations*. Kim blogs at www.magnoliabayquilts.blogspot.com.

LYNN RODDY BROWN

Lynn is a sixth-generation Texan who has always loved to sew. For more than 10 years, she's belonged to a bee that trades blocks for scrap quilts; this experience evolved into her first book, *Simple Strategies for Block-Swap Quilts*. Lynn's third book will be released in 2011.

KAY CONNORS and KAREN EARLYWINE

Sisters whose lifelong love of quilting comes from their talented grandmothers, Kay and Karen have coauthored two books, *Link to the '30s: Making the Quilts We Didn't Inherit* and *Fancy to Frugal: Authentic Quilt Patterns from the '30s*.

KIM DIEHL

Kim's warm style and distinctive pieced and appliquéd designs have turned her five books into top sellers. Her most recent release is *Simple Graces: Charming Quilts and Companion Projects*.

MIMI DIETRICH

A nationally known teacher, Mimi is the author of 15 quilting books, including one of Martingale & Company's all-time bestsellers, *Happy Endings*. Visit Mimi at www.mimidietrich.com.

JOANNA FIGUEROA

A busy mother of three, Joanna somehow finds time to create quilts for her books and pattern line, design fabric, write a regular magazine column, and keep up a creative online journal called Fresh Figs (www.figtreequilts.typepad.com).

JUDY HOPKINS

Judy's fondness for traditional design goes hand in hand with an unwavering commitment to fast, contemporary cutting and piecing techniques. She has authored more than 15 books and designed countless patterns.

NANCY MAHONEY

Nancy estimates that in her 20-plus years of quiltmaking, she's made more than 400 quilts! She's authored 10 books, including bestsellers *Quilt Revival* and *Appliqué Quilt Revival*. Learn more at www.nancymahoney.com.

NANCY J. MARTIN

Founder of Martingale & Company, Nancy is also the author of more than 40 books. Her titles have sold over a million copies to date. Visit her at www.nancysgreengarden.com and http://ja-jp.facebook.com/gardeninggourmet.

CLAUDIA PLETT and LE ANN WEAVER

Claudia and Le Ann met in 2002 when they were both making a mystery quilt on an Internet quilting forum. Their love of designing with precut 5" and 10" squares led them to coauthor two bestselling books, *Loose Change: Quilts from Nickels, Dimes, and Fat Quarters* and *More Loose Change*.

SALLY SCHNEIDER

Having made several hundred quilts since she began quilting in 1971, Sally is confident that none of her children or grandchildren will ever go cold at night! Sally has authored eight books for Martingale & Company. Learn more at www.sallyschneider.com.

EVELYN SLOPPY

Evelyn believes there's no better way to give back to her community than by doing what she loves to do—make quilts. That's why she makes and donates dozens of charity quilts each year. Evelyn has authored five quilting books.

PAT SPETH

Pat had quilters everywhere cutting their fabric into 5" squares with the publication of her first book, *Nickel Quilts*, in 2002. She's since written three more books on the subject. Learn more at www.patspeth.com.

CYNDI WALKER

Cyndi has a degree in fashion art and advertising. She currently enjoys teaching, designing fabrics, and designing quilts for her pattern company, Stitch Studios (www.stitchstudios.com). Cyndi blogs at www.wishfulstitches.com.

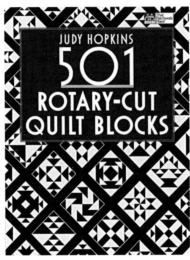
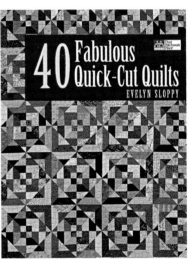

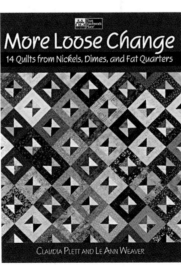
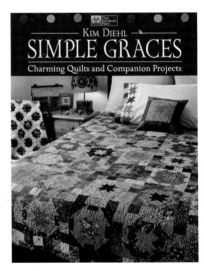